TWENTIETH CENTURY SERIES

PROPHET OF A BROKEN HOME

An Exposition of Hosea

By

FREDK. A. TATFORD

1974

PROPHETIC WITNESS PUBLISHING HOUSE

Upperton House, ⟨...⟩ Sussex, BN21 3YB

Printed by Errey's Printers, High Street, Heathfield, Sussex.

TWENTIETH CENTURY SERIES

CONTENTS

PREFACE

SOME three years ago the author was induced to put into print a series of lectures which he had given on the Prophecy of Zechariah. It was immediately suggested by a colleague, who succeeded in securing the support of the Council of the Prophetic Witness Movement International for the idea, that this should be the first of a series of books on the Minor Prophets.

Literary commitments and preaching engagements, coupled with the editorship of two magazines, made one extremely reluctant to attempt such a task, but eventually a second volume saw the light of day—an exposition of Malachi. With the present volume on Hosea, the task is completed and all twelve books have been published. It says much for the patience of the author's wife that it has been possible to fulfil the commitment, and it is hoped that some readers will benefit from the result.

A great deal of study and research has gone into the preparation of the books and an attempt has been made to give the accurate meaning of the text. The author has probably received more benefit from the work than any who later read the books.

FREDK. A. TATFORD.

CHAPTER 1

Introduction

A CONTEMPORARY of Amos and Isaiah, Hosea was a native of the northern kingdom of Israel. This is evident from his obviously intimate knowledge of the political and religious conditions of that nation, his historical and topographical allusions, and the northern dialectical peculiarities which the linguistic experts profess to discover in the language he employed. There are many incidental confirmations of the fact, e.g. his reference in ch. 7 : 5 to "our king". His ministry, moreover, was plainly directly primarily to Israel, although he made occasional references to Judah.

Nothing is known of the prophet except what is contained in his book. His name meant "salvation", and it was identical with that of the last king of Israel (2 Kings 15 : 30) and with the original name of Joshua before he was renamed by Moses (Num. 13 : 8, 16). It was also the name of one of the princes of Ephraim in David's day (1 Chron. 27 : 20) and of one of the chiefs who sealed the covenant in Nehemiah's day (Neh. 10 : 23).

The prophet is said by some commentators to have originated from Behemoth in the tribe of Issachar and to have died and been buried at his native town, but other traditions maintain that his father was a Reubenite. A Jewish legend states that he died and was buried at Babylon, but his grave is also said to be at Safed in Upper Galilee, although another grave at Ramoth-Gilead, east of Jordan, is claimed to be his.

There is, in fact, no reliable information regarding his tribe, birthplace, or burial site.

Because of his frequent references to the priests, the temple, the festivals, the offerings and the law, it has been suggested by Duhm and others that Hosea belonged to the priestly order, but this conjecture is without substantial support. Indeed, the manner in which he addressed the priests tends to imply that he was distinct from them. If he belonged to the Levitical tribe, questions might well arise regarding his long neglect of his sacerdotal functions and his absence from Jerusalem, but there is no justification for the theory of his priestly connection. His condemnations of the priests, of the golden calves and Baal would rule out any likelihood of his being associated with either of those priesthoods.

His book makes it clear that the prophet was closely acquainted with the agricultural life. Many of his symbols and illustrations were patently drawn therefrom. As George Adam Smith (*The Book of the Twelve Prophets,* vol. 1, p. 233) remarks, "With Hosea we feel all the seasons of the Syrian year: early rain and latter rain, the first flush of the young corn, the scent of the vine blossom, the first ripe fig of the fig tree in her first season, the bursting of the lily; the wild vine trailing on the hedge, the field of tares, the beauty of the full olive in sunshine and breeze; the mists and heavy dews of a summer morning in Ephraim, the night winds laden with the air of the mountains, the scent of Lebanon. Or is it the clearer human sights in valley and field : the smoke from the chimney, the chaff from the threshing-floor, the doves startled to their towers, the fowler and his net; the breaking up of the fallow ground, the harrowing of the clods, the reapers, the heifer that treadeth out the corn; the team of draught oxen surmounting the steep road, and at the top the kindly driver setting in food to their jaws." The book is, in fact, redolent of the countryside.

At the same time, it is probable that Hosea belonged to the wealthier class of the community. The language he used, the character of his allusions, and the similes, metaphors and other figures of speech which he employed, imply that he was a man of considerable ability, learning and culture.

He was evidently called to the prophetic office at a fairly early age. He had presumably not long attained marriageable age when the event which initiated his ministry occurred and he was divinely directed to take a wife to himself.

Since his ministry extended from the days of Uzziah to those of Hezekiah, Pusey (not very accurately) estimates that he prophesied for a period of approximately 70 years and that he consequently lived to an advanced age. Certainly tradition supports the theory that he enjoyed a long life, but the exact period of his public activities can be deduced only from the details given in chapter 1 : 1, and these do not indicate the precise dates of the commencement and conclusion of his ministry.

It is commonly thought that, in his later years (possibly after the fall of Samaria), Hosea retired to Judah and that he there committed his prophecies to writing. Many critics maintain that the prophet's writings were brought together and revised by an editor from Judah and that this redactor was responsible for a number of interpolations, but it is more probable that the whole of the book was compiled by the prophet himself.

That Hosea was a strong character can scarcely be doubted. Ewald opines that he was compelled to contend with the most violent hostility as well as with secret plots. He courageously resisted contemporaneous trends and attitudes and, despite the evident opposition, vigorously attacked the practices, motifs and rubrics of the popular fertility cult. With a deep personal experience of sorrow, he entered into the feelings of the God of Israel and, to an extent unparalleled by any other prophet, exposed the love of Jehovah for His people. He was unquestionably a man of keen spiritual discernment and of intense devotion to God and His people.

BACKGROUND

The period during which Hosea lived and prophesied was

one of considerable material and political prosperity. Joash and Jeroboam II had succeeded in recovering the cities lost earlier to Syria, in annexing Damascus, and in restoring the boundaries of Israel from Hamath to the Dead Sea. Despite the apparent prosperity, however, there was a moral and spiritual decline, and the shadows of impending trouble were already gathering on the horizon. God had promised Jehu that his "sons of the fourth generation should sit on the throne of Israel" (2 Kings 15 : 12), and Jeroboam's son, Zechariah, was the last of the dynasty and his rule was limited to six months (2 Kings 15 : 8). The subsequent history of the kingdom was virtually a military despotism, misrule and anarchy.

The spiritual condition of the people was deplorably low, and corruption was widespread. This was largely due to Israel's adoption of the Canaanite religion and the syncretistic modification of Judaism under the influence of Baalism.

When Jeroboam I rebelled against Rehoboam and became ruler of the ten tribes of Israel, he had golden images of calves placed in sanctuaries at Bethel and Dan and a priesthood appointed for their service, in order that the people might be diverted from the temple at Jerusalem and from its services and festivals. Initially the calves were intended merely as a representation of Jehovah, but they subsequently became associated with the worship of Baal. After Ahab's marriage with Jezebel, Baalism was introduced into Israel and Ahab built a temple for Baal at Samaria, although he still counted himself a follower of Jehovah. Jehu later rooted out Baalism from Israel, but still retained the golden calves, so that the people naturally reverted eventually to the worship of Baal.

Baal (which means "lord" or "owner") was a generic title for "god" in the Semitic languages and it was applied to many deities and even to Jehovah. David named one of his sons Beeliada or Eliada (1 Chron. 14 : 7; 2 Sam. 5 : 16), indicating that Baal was regarded as equivalent to El, while one of his captains was named Bealiah (1 Chron. 12 : 5), which means "Jehovah is Baal".

Said to be the son of Dagon, Baal was considered the most important deity in the Canaanite pantheon. Tablets discovered in 1929 onwards at Ras Shamra (the ancient Ugarit) in northern Syria, which date from the second millennium B.C., have provided a great deal of information about the god. He was described as the god of rain and storm and the source of all the blessings of nature. The fertility of the land, flocks, herds and even the family was allegedly a boon bestowed by him: consequently the firstfruits were a tribute to be paid to him. His worship demanded incense (Jer. 7 : 9), animal and human sacrifice (Jer. 19 : 5), bowing and kissing, sacred cakes, grossly licentious practices and sacred prostitution.

As Baal was the supreme male divinity of the Phoenicians, Ashtoreth or Astarte was the supreme female deity; she was usually represented as a nude woman, astride a lion, with a lily in one hand and a serpent in the other. This goddess, who was originally known as Anat, was the sister and consort of Baal. The latter was said to die every summer, slain by Mot, the god of drought and of the nether world. But the powerful Anat, in turn, slew Mot and thereby put an end to the drought. Baal, the god of rain, immediately rose from the dead to cover the land with the beneficial showers so badly needed. Ashtoreth was regarded as the goddess of fertility and reproduction and was equated with the planet Venus. Solomon built a "high place" for her at Jerusalem, which was later desecrated by Josiah (1 Kings 11 : 5; 2 Kings 23 : 13).

A feature of the idolatrous religion which grew up around Baal and Ashtoreth was the erection by the altar of a stone pillar (*mazzebah*) in honour of the former, and of a wooden pole (*asherah*) as a symbol of the latter, both of which symbolised human fertility and the first of which had a phallic significance. Chambers and wooded areas were reserved for the sacred prostitution associated with the worship, male prostitutes (*kedishim*) being consecrated to Ashtoreth, and sacred harlots (*kedeshoth*) to Baal (1 Kings 14 : 23, 24; 15 : 12; 22 : 46; 2 Kings 23 : 7; Hos. 4 : 14).

In an agrarian society the productivity of the land, flocks

and herds was of the utmost importance. Israel occupied Jehovah's land and their agricultural prosperity was attributable to His beneficence. But before long they were following the example of their heathen neighbours and ascribing the gifts of the land to Baal. At first they merely used the name in relation to Jehovah Himself, but gradually there developed the recognition of a separate deity or deities (Baal and the Baalim of various localities) and consequently the adoption of the Canaanite system of worship.

Basic to the cult of Baal and Ashtoreth was the concept of ensuring the fecundity of land, animals and humans through the release of a supernatural procreative power by the cosmic sexual union of the god and goddess. This was allegedly precipitated by the sacral union of the cultic prostitute with a devotee of the opposite sex. This was no sexual orgy, but a deliberate act of worship to secure the desired temporal benefits. In the licentious dancing following the ritualistic meal of the cult, however, sensuality often ran riot and unrestrained licence resulted in polluting promiscuity. Among those who remained loyal to Jehovah, there developed a tendency to refer contemptuously to the idolatrous cult as a shame (*bosheth*)—an assessment in complete agreement with the condemnation of the prophets.

Baalism was widespread: temples and altars were erected, for example, by Ahab (1 Kings 16 : 32) and large numbers of priests (described as *kemarim* because of their black garments) served the deity. Eight hundred and fifty who served Baal and Ashtoreth, for instance, were slain at Elijah's confrontation on Carmel (1 Kings 18 : 19–40). The terms Baal and Ashtoreth were frequently used of deities of particular locales, and the Old Testament often uses the plural, Baalim and Ashteroth, because of the multiplicity of such local deities. This idolatrous system was that with which Israel of Hosea's day was completely entangled and against which the prophet so vehemently inveighed.

The adoption of the idolatry of Baalism had borne bitter fruit in the lives of the people. To quote E. B. Pusey (*The*

Minor Prophets, vol. 1, p. 12), "Every commandment of God was broken, and that habitually. All was falsehood, adultery, bloodshedding; deceit to God produced faithlessness to man; excess and luxury were supplied by secret or open robbery, oppression, false dealing, perversion of justice, grinding of the poor. Blood was shed like water . . . Adultery was consecrated as an act of religion. Those who were first in rank were first in excess. People and king vied in debauchery, and the sottish king joined and encouraged the freethinkers and blasphemers of his court. The idolatrous priests loved and shared in the sins of the people; nay, they seem to have set themselves to intercept those on either side of Jordan, who would go to worship at Jerusalem, laying wait to murder them. Corruption had spread throughout the whole land . . . Remonstrance was useless; the knowledge of God was wilfully rejected; the people hated rebuke." It seems almost incredible that the declension should have been so swift and so extensive. Yet the moral and spiritual deterioration which has occurred in our twentieth century is even greater in extent and has happened more rapidly.

DATE

According to Hos. 1 : 1, the prophet's ministry spanned the reigns of Uzziah, Jotham, Ahaz and Hezekiah, kings of Judah, and of Jeroboam II, king of Israel. Jeroboam II reigned from 782 to 745 B.C., his reign overlapping that of Uzziah (or Azariah), who reigned from 791 to 740 B.C. and was followed by Jotham, Ahaz and Hezekiah, the last reigning from 721 to 686 B.C. Hosea, therefore, commenced prophesying some time after 782 B.C. and concluded before 686 B.C. From his description of the conditions of the country, it is thought that he probably started his ministry about 750 B.C. and that his activities continued until after the fall of Samaria in 721 B.C. Ibn Ezra claimed that he prophesied from 760 to 721 B.C.

The first three chapters may clearly be dated in Jeroboam's reign, since the end of the dynasty of Jehu, which occurred in 745 B.C. with the murder of Zechariah by the usurper Shallum, was predicted as a still future event (ch. 1 : 4). The conditions of Jeroboam's reign were reflected in the details given in these chapters. The particulars given in the remaining chapters could well be applicable to Jeroboam's day or to the period which followed, and this section of the book cannot therefore be so readily dated.

STYLE

Patently the product of the educated class, Hosea was unique among the Minor Prophets for the style and range of his phraseology. S. M. Lehrman (*Hosea*, p. 1) says, "His language is characterised by a classical style, compactness of period and fervour of utterance." From polemic and apologetic, he soared into flights of poetry or descended into the bathos of grief, only to revert once more to forceful and logical argument.

He employed metaphor and simile in rich profusion and multiplied illustrations to reinforce the impact of his words. The frequent use of paronomasia, or play upon words, was characteristic of his speech, although this is often lost in the English translation. In the variety of his imagery, it is not always easy today, moreover, to determine the significance of some of his cryptic allusions and subtle innuendos.

His unhappy marital experience clearly affected the whole character of his preaching. With amazing insight, he saw his own experience as a reflection of Jehovah's and condemned Israel for her spiritual adultery, contemptuously referring to the false deities she worshipped as her illicit lovers, who provided her with a prostitute's hire in the form of grain, oil and wine. His wife's infidelity coloured his book. "Exhaustless is the sorrow," wrote Ewald (*The Prophets,* vol. 1, p. 128), "endless the grief wherever the mind turns, and ever and anon the tossing restless discourse begins again, like the wild cry of an anguish that can hardly be mastered." It is no wonder that, in his intense determination to re-establish the aniconic purity of the worship of Jehovah, he scathingly denounced the mythology of Baal.

CANONICITY

Although controversy continues regarding Hosea's authorship of the whole of the book as it stands and as regards the alleged part played by Judean editors, it is generally accepted that the contents represent prophecies uttered by Hosea and subsequently committed to writing by him. It is sometimes argued that chapter 14 was added by another author and that the substitution of Judah for Israel was made in some places by a later editor, but this is pure speculation. Most conservative scholars today accept the unity and authorship of the book.

No serious doubt has ever been raised regarding its inspiration or canonicity. Its place as first of the Minor Prophets was probably due to its size rather than to the date of production: it was not, of course, chronologically the first.

CONTENTS

Hosea obviously delivered a large number of addresses to the people of Israel—some of which he doubtless repeated—but, in compiling the book which bears his name, he did not record each message separately, but seems rather to have given a summary of the principal points made in his addresses. On the fall of Samaria, he presumably made his way south to Judah, where his writings were subsequently preserved. Whether or not he continued his ministry in the southern kingdom, there is no indication.

After the story of the domestic tragedy contained in the first three chapters, the greater part of the book is concerned with the moral and spiritual corruption of the people, upon whom the earlier words of Amos had apparently had no effect. The prophet castigated the priests, whose duty it was to teach the precepts of the law and the morality implicit therein, but who had not only grossly failed to inculcate the principles of the *torah*, but had encouraged the prevalent immorality and iniquity for their own gain. He denounced the sinfulness, vacillation and weakness of the royal house and of the rulers generally, and poured scorn upon the political intrigues and futile negotiations with Assyria and Egypt. He warned of the inevitable judgment which must fall upon a guilty nation for its apostasy and the bitter experience of exile which was now inescapable.

The conclusion of the prophecy is a remarkable piece of literature. To quote R. F. Horton (*The Minor Prophets,* vol. 1, p. 12), "The book ends with an appeal, passionate and tender, in which the voices of the prophet and of God and of the repentant people form a great amoebean symphony. The fall of the nation, and the deposition of the apostate kings, are forgotten, and nothing remains but that eternal and spiritual drama transacted between the soul and God, which is the underlying substance and the over-arching purpose of all Holy Scripture."

The book may be analysed as follows,
1. Superscription (1 : 1).
2. Israel's infidelity (1 : 2 — 3 : 5).
3. Moral decay (4 : 1 — 7 : 7).
4. Political decay (7 : 8 — 10 : 15).
5. Jehovah's love (11 : 1–12).
6. Divine anger (12 : 1 — 13 : 16).
7. Call to repentance (14 : 1–9).

NEW TESTAMENT QUOTATIONS

The prophecy of Hosea is quoted at least nine times in the New Testament, viz.,

Hos. 1 : 9, 10 in Rom. 9 : 25, 26; 1 Pet. 2 : 10.
Hos. 2 : 23 in Rom. 9 : 25; 1 Pet. 2 : 10.
Hos. 6 : 6 in Matt. 9 : 13; 12 : 7.
Hos. 10 : 8 in Luke 23 : 30.
Hos. 11 : 1 in Matt. 2 : 15.
Hos. 13 : 14 in 1 Cor. 15 : 55.

In the Old Testament it is evident that Jeremiah was intimately acquainted with the contents of the book, and his own writings repeatedly reflect those of the earlier prophet.

CHAPTER 2

An Unhappy Marriage

THE northern kingdom of Israel probably reached its greatest glory during the reign of Jeroboam II, the great grandson of Jehu, one of the most outstanding rulers of the ten tribes. After his death the descent into anarchy and ultimate captivity was rapid. To the discerning eye of a spiritual man, however, the evidences of decay were already apparent in Jeroboam's day, and the voice of a young man was lifted up to awaken the conscience and bring conviction to the people.

THE CALL

The word of Jehovah that came to Hosea, the son of Beeri, in the days of Uzziah, Jotham, Ahaz and Hezekiah, kings of Judah, and in the days of Jeroboam, the son of Joash, king of Israel (Hos. 1 : 1).

The similarity of the superscription of several of the prophetic books of the Bible has led some to conclude that this indicated the hand of circles who edited these books during the exilic and post-exilic periods, but this is not necessarily the case. The words may well have been those of the prophet himself. "The word of Jehovah" was a term used in the case of eight of the Minor Prophets (Hosea, Joel, Jonah, Micah, Zephaniah, Haggai, Zechariah and Malachi). It was an unquestionable authentication of the contents of the book: what followed was not the word of the human messenger but the inspired declaration of God Himself.

Hosea described himself as the son of Beeri, but gave no further information regarding his lineage, profession or tribe. His own name meant "salvation" and his father's "belonging to the well", but this does not assist in identification. The only other Beeri mentioned in the Bible was the Hittite whose daughter was one of Esau's wives (Gen. 26 : 34). He has been identified by some writers with Beerah, the Reubenite prince carried away captive by Tiglath-pileser (1 Chron. 5 : 6): this is not impossible. One tradition states that Beeri was also a prophet and that Isa. 8 : 19–22 represents one of his prophecies which Isaiah incorported in his own book: this is less likely. If his father was the Beerah who was exiled to Assyria, Hosea came of a noble family.

It is sometimes thought strange that a prophet of Israel should date his prophecy by reference to kings of Judah, as well as by the then king of Israel. This may well be explicable by the prophet's conviction that the separation of the ten tribes was virtually apostasy and that the legitimate rulers of God's people were still the kings of Judah. Hosea's ministry extended over a long period. Keil, in fact, estimates that he prophesied for between 60 and 65 years (27 to 30 years under Uzziah, 31 under Jotham and Ahaz, and 1 to 3 years under Hezekiah). He certainly must have occupied the prophetic office for 30 to 40 years and possibly for much longer. Keil's figures for Jotham and Ahaz are on the high side.

THE HARLOT WIFE

When Jehovah spoke at first with Hosea, Jehovah said to Hosea, Go, take to yourself a wife of harlotry and children of harlotry: for the land commits great harlotry by forsaking Jehovah (Hos. 1 : 2).

Before Hosea actually commenced to prophesy, he was divinely instructed to acquire a wife. There was no official call to the ministry: this was his first public act. But it was one of the utmost significance. One writer says that "the essential catalyst for the mediation of God's word was the personal crisis associated with Hosea's marriage and children." As in the case of Ezekiel, God used the prophet's own life and experiences to illustrate the Divine message.

The command was a strange one, "Go and take to yourself a wife of harlotry and children of harlotry". Was the prophet then to marry one of the sacred prostitutes of the fertility cult or, alternatively, a woman who habitually committed adultery and was steeped in sin? Had it been intended that he should marry an adulteress, the expression used would have been different (*ishah zonah*). It seems rather that his bride was to be one who either had a deep-seated inclination to adultery already or who would eventually lapse into sexual sin for some reason.

Not only is it improbable that Jehovah would command marriage with a prostitute or with a woman of an unchaste disposition, but it would have been inconsistent with His purpose. Hosea's wife was to symbolise Israel as the wife of Jehovah. The Israel whom God originally espoused was innocent and was devoted to Him (Jer. 2 : 2); it was only subsequently that she became unfaithful because of the seductions of a false religion. Similarly, as another has said, "The struggle of Hosea's shame and grief when he found his wife unfaithful is altogether inconceivable unless his first love had been pure and full of trust in the purity of its object."

If the view is taken that Hosea was unaware of the true character of his wife and of how disastrous his marriage would become, it must be assumed that the Divine words recorded in verse 2 were either not understood or were not uttered at the time. Was it perhaps only later that the prophet realised the significance of Jehovah's command? In retrospect he could realise why he had been directed to marry and, with the deep insight acquired, could appreciate the experiences of God with Israel. As Smith (*op. cit.*, p. 238) says, when, years later, the character of his wife had become evident, Hosea "pushed back his own knowledge of God's purpose to the date when

20

that purpose began actually to be fulfilled, the day of his betrothal. This, though he was all unconscious of the fatal future, had been to Hosea the beginning of the word of the Lord."

God also disclosed to the prophet that his marriage was symbolic: it was a parallel of the adultery committed by the land (as figurative of the nation) in forsaking Jehovah. The gods of the heathen were commonly described as married to the land of their followers or to the nation which acknowledged them. Jehovah took up the language of the heathen and declared by implication that He was married to Israel—both land and nation. If Hosea's wife was unfaithful to him, it was but a pale reflection of Israel's infidelity to Jehovah. Hosea was the first of the prophets to use such daring symbolism, although he was later followed by Jeremiah and Ezekiel.

JEZREEL

So he went and took Gomer, the daughter of Diblaim; who conceived and bore him a son. And Jehovah said to him, Call his name Jezreel. For yet a little while and I will punish the house of Jehu for the blood of Jezreel, and will bring to an end the kingdom of the house of Israel. And on that day I will break the bow of Israel in the valley of Jezreel (Hos. 1 : 3-5).

Hosea did not demur to the Divine command. He went and took Gomer (which means "perfection"), the daughter of Diblaim (i.e. "cakes of figs") as his wife. There are not wanting expositors who insist that Hosea's marriage was not actual but allegorical. This can hardly be accepted. The names of Gomer and Diblaim have no real significance in the narrative, whereas it would be reasonable to expect names with a typical meaning to be employed if the story was simply an allegory. In addition, details such as the birth and weaning of the child substantiate the historicity of the account. Gomer

21

bat Diblaim was a literal woman whom the prophet actually married.

Gomer conceived and bore a son to Hosea. It is significant that verse 3 states that she "bore *him* a son", whereas the word "him" is omitted in verses 6 and 8. No adulterous propensity was evident at this stage. The first child was Hosea's own son. The child was named, however, by Jehovah. Four times in chapter 1 Jehovah spoke to the prophet to reveal His purpose to him. As has well been said, we cannot speak for God unless we have first heard His voice to us. Dietrich Bonhoeffer pertinently remarked, "I could not preach if I did not know that I speak God's word, and I could not preach if I did not know that I cannot speak God's word. Human impossibility and Divine promise are one."

The firstborn son was to be named Jezreel (i.e. "God sows"). The valley of Jezreel, lying between the mountain ranges of Galilee and Samaria, was a well-watered plain and one of the most fertile areas in the country. It was, in fact, so productive that it was said that it was sown by Jehovah, whence it acquired its name. It was at the town of Jezreel, on the southern edge of the valley, that Jehu slew Jehoram and Jezebel of Israel, Ahaziah of Judah and the princes of Israel (2 Kings 9 : 24 to 10 : 11), going on to massacre the princes of Judah and the worshippers of Baal. The deceit and bloody deeds of Jehu, although primarily in fulfilment of the Divine purpose, went beyond the commission given him by Elisha (2 Kings 9 : 7), since no mention had been made of Judah, and they were generally viewed with abhorrence and God granted him but four generations to sit on his throne. Now punishment must come and the fruitful valley of Jezreel would be sown with destruction for the descendants of Jehu. God takes account of men's actions and eventually the day of reckoning must come.

The dynasty of Jehu was to end with the murder of Zechariah, and Hosea associated the end of the kingdom of Israel with that event, although that did not occur for another decade. It is possible that the prophet referred to the invasion of Tiglath-pileser III in 733 B.C. (2 Kings 15 : 29), but he probably also anticipated a still future day when the tides of battle will once more flow across the fertile valley of Jezreel or Esdraelon, culminating in the last great battle at Megiddo. The name given to Hosea's son was the constant reminder of the unfailing purpose of God.

"On that day" (an eschatological term), declared Jehovah, He would break the bow of Israel in the valley of Jezreel. (There is, of course, a paronomasia between Israel and Jezreel here). The whole of the military power of Israel was to be destroyed in Jezreel. The ruthless invasion of Tiglath-pileser and the consequent vassalage of Israel were only a fore-shadowing of what is still to come. Israel has still a day of trouble to face, when all her confidence in military might will be destroyed and God will prove His word in the valley of Jezreel (Zech. 14 : 1, 2; Rev. 16 : 16).

LORUHAMAH

And she conceived again and bore a daughter. And Jehovah said to him, Call her name Lo-ruhamah: for I will no longer have compassion on the house of Israel, that I should in any wise pardon them. But I will have compassion on the house of Judah, and will deliver them by Jehovah their Elohim, and will not deliver them by bow, nor by sword, nor by battle, nor by horses, nor by horsemen (Hos.1 : 6, 7).

The second child born to Gomer was apparently illegitimate and Hosea obviously became aware of his wife's infidelity. Although he did not put her away, as he might justifiably have done, his disillusionment was evident. At the Divine command he named Gomer's daughter Lo-ruhamah, meaning "without pity or compassion". Marital love and domestic peace had gone; while he provided a home for the child, he could not play the paternal role to her. He had no compassion for her; there was no pity in his heart; she was the cause of the scandal which must now have become public.

Yet the sorrows of his life were being utilised by God to

illustrate His relations with Israel. Her perfidy was equally as great, and the name given to Gomer's daughter was to serve as an indication that He would no longer have compassion upon the nation. Her treachery to her Maker-Husband had dried up the wells of Divine mercy. Jehovah's favour was no longer set upon her and He offered no pardon or forgiveness for her wrongdoing. Irretrievable disaster was implicit in the words. The destiny of the kingdom was now determined and in a few decades the nation was to be scattered and its territory confiscated. "It is an awful moment when we find that we have drifted beyond the mercies of God," says one writer, but it is only too sadly possible even today. God is infinitely holy and cannot tolerate sin. If the backslider persists in his course, he will eventually deprive himself of the mercy and goodness of God.

Then extraordinarily, Jehovah declared that He would have compassion on the house of Judah and would Himself deliver them, not by military weapons or conflict but inferentially by His own power. The reference is almost undoubtedly to the miraculous deliverance of Jerusalem in 701 B.C. The army of Sennacherib invaded Judah but, as Isaiah promised, the Assyrian host was routed—not as the result of battle nor by the military might of Hezekiah, but by the hand of God. The angel of Jehovah slew 185,000 Assyrians in the night (2 Kings 19 : 35).

It is strange that a prediction regarding Judah should have been inserted at this point and the New English Bible relegates verse 7 to a footnote. The critics insist that the verse was an interpolation by an editor of Judah, some even claiming that it was inserted by Hezekiah himself. But it is doubtful whether Judah was aware of this particular prophecy. It was probably uttered by Hosea to Israel to emphasise the difference in God's dealings with Judah and thereby to awaken Israel to a realisation of her own situation.

LOAMMI
Now when she had weaned Lo-ruhamah, she conceived and

24

bore a son. Then said Jehovah, Call his name Lo-ammi: for you are not my people and I will not be your God (Hos. 1 : 8, 9).

The tragedy was not yet played out, for another child of adultery was born. In the Middle East at that time, it was not customary for a child to be weaned before it was at least two years old and sometimes three years. The occasion then was one for feasting and celebration (Gen. 21 : 8). When Gomer's daughter had been weaned, she again conceived and a second son was born.

Once again it was evident to her longsuffering husband that the child was not his and this was made even clearer in the name bestowed upon him at God's command. He was to be named Lo-ammi, which means "not my people". Again Jehovah indicated that the name was symbolic, for He applied it to Israel and declared that they were not His people and that He would not be their God. This was the very antithesis of the covenant promise of an earlier day (Ex. 6 : 7; Deut. 26 : 17, 18) and disclosed the extent of the breach between Israel and their God.

Gomer must have lived with Hosea for some six years, but his shame was now exposed to all. Yet, as his prophecy makes clear, there must have been a large number of homes in Israel in which similar conditions existed. The anguish of the prophet taught him not only perception but sympathy and understanding. Yet these conditions were but a reflection of the spiritual relationship between Israel and Jehovah and he was being taught the greater story of the sorrow of the Divine heart at the waywardness of a nation which had enjoyed such great favour. Israel had brought illegitimate offspring into being in the form of their idolatrous practices and worship, and had been spiritually unfaithful to God.

Gomer's children were a standing rebuke to the nation and a constant reminder of God's repudiation of His people. The naming of the children and the public explanation of the reasons therefor must have required great courage on the part

25

of the prophet. Luxury, idolatry, immorality and oppression were the accepted pattern of the day, and Hosea's preaching must have been extremely unpalatable. But if the message was stern, it was proclaimed by a sorrowing man, whose mercy to his wife had extended over six years and had ignored her unfaithfulness. The preacher was a man of compassion and understanding, albeit of unyielding purpose and conviction.

The lesson is one which would well be conned over today. In many so-called Christian circles there is as much unfaithfulness to God as in Hosea's day. Those who deny the fundamental truths of the Bible yet claim to be Christians can scarcely expect the Omniscient to ignore their rejection. Those who compromise with the world which crucified Christ and tolerate evil within the church are only invoking a Divine repudiation. The President of a large American denomination has been a member of the Communist party for 26 years: how can the member of an atheistic organisation escape the hand of judgment? In *World Without Change* Kurt Koch tells of what he describes as "the most popular party game in some churches". He says, "After the evening service, married couples who have been in church meet in the church basement and sit in a circle. Then they begin a party game which is called key throwing. The men throw a key to one of the women. If she catches it, then they sleep together that night. If she does not catch the key, it means she refuses him as a partner. It is, of course, the attractive women who have most keys thrown to them. The less fortunate ladies must wait to the end, until someone takes pity on them and throws them the key." Were the practices of Israel 2,700 years ago any more deserving of condemnation? A holy God cannot tolerate sin and we do well to take heed to Hosea's warning of centuries ago.

A RENEWED COVENANT

Yet the number of the people of Israel shall be like the sand of the sea, which cannot be measured or numbered; and it shall come to pass that, in the place where it was said to

26

*them, You are not my people, it shall be said to them, Sons of
the living God (El). Then shall the people of Judah and the
people of Israel be gathered together, and they shall appoint
one head for themselves, and they shall go up from the land:
for great shall be the day of Jezreel (Hos. 1 : 10, 11).*

Verses 10 and 11 of Hos. 1 form the first two verses of
chapter 2 in the Hebrew Bible. Their contents are such a glar-
ing contradiction of the preceding verses that the critics maintain that the verses were an interpolation by an exilic editor.
There is, however, no reason for not attributing the words to
Hosea himself, since it is not the only occasion in his book
where there is a sudden and unexpected transition—in this
case, from judgment to mercy—and it cannot be claimed in
every instance that the words were inserted by another hand.

Despite the rejection intimated in verse 9, Jehovah reiterated the promise given to Abraham that his descendants, the
people of Israel, should be as numberless as the sand on the
sea-shore, the grains of which could never be counted (Gen.
22 : 17). The covenant with the patriarch was an uncondi-
tional and irrevocable one: nothing could annul it (Gal. 3 :
17). The sin of Israel merited—and received—punishment,
but God had bound Himself by oath to implement that
covenant. Appropriately, therefore, the prophet reverted to it,
after pronouncing the judgment which had been invoked, in
order to assure the people of the immutability of the Divine
purpose and the faithfulness of God in spite of their unfaithfulness.

Moreover, in the very place in which the people had been
told of the severance of Jehovah's relationship with them, they
would one day be called "sons of the living God". The Divine
purpose would be fulfilled irrespective of the sin and failure of
Israel. The apostle Paul audaciously applied Hosea's words,
not only to the faithful remnant of Israel but to Gentile be-
lievers in the Christian era, in the course of his argument in
Rom. 9 : 25, 26. Peter, equally daringly, applied the words
specifically to Christians (1 Pet. 2 : 10). Neither apostle was,

27

of course, interpreting the sayings of Hosea, but merely using the expressions as illustrative of the particular points being made.

The purpose of God was even more far-reaching. It was His plan that the schism of the centuries should be healed, and that Israel and Judah should be reunited. One day they will be gathered together and, according to the prophet, will then appoint one head as their ruler. According to Ibn Ezra, who patently did not realise the implication, this referred to Sennacherib, but Rashi and Kimchi more logically maintained that the reference was to David. It would perhaps be more accurate to say that the one envisioned was "great David's greater Son", for the future ruler of the combined nation of Israel will be no other than our Lord Jesus Christ.

When that day dawns, the exiles will evacuate the lands of their dispersion and go up once more to Zion. From all points of the compass they will return to the promised land. In that day, Jezreel will have a totally different significance. The memory of Jehu's massacre will fade away, and the valley once sown with the seeds of vengeance and destruction will be sown by God with the seeds of lasting blessing. "Great shall be the day of Jezreel," said the prophet. The superabounding grace of Jehovah will sweep over all hindrances and transform the great valley into a scene of fruitfulness once again.

Already Israel has returned to her own land in unbelief. Millions more Jews are still in dispersion, but the rivulet which has started must inevitably swell into a mighty torrent. The Divine purpose must be achieved.

CHAPTER 3

Rebuke and Restoration

THE tragedy of Hosea's home afforded the opportunity for God to disclose the greater tragedy of Israel's unfaithfulness and the inescapable necessity for putting the wheels of justice in motion. Her conduct could not be tolerated indefinitely and her blatant sin inevitably attracted judgment. The language used by the prophet, although appropriate initially to his own marital circumstances, went far beyond the characters of his own home: indeed, many of the details he quoted had no direct relevance to his wife or his family. His experiences were merely employed by God as illustrative of the nation and their relationship to Him.

CALLED TO ACCOUNT

Say to your brothers, Ammi, and to your sisters, Ruhamah, Contend with your mother, contend. For she is not my wife, neither am I her husband. Let her, therefore, put away her harlotry from her face, and her adultery from between her breasts, Lest I strip her naked and make her as in the day that she was born, and make her like a wilderness and make her like a parched land, and slay her with thirst (Hos. 2 : 1–3).

Hosea had been directed to name Gomer's second son Lo-Ammi and her daughter Lo-Ruhamah, but now he called to the people, naming them Ammi (i.e. my people) and

Ruhamah (i.e. compassion). That his words were not addressed to his own children was evident from the fact that he used the plural words, "brothers" and "sisters". He commanded them to contend with their mother: the faithful remnant in the land were to enter into the controversy with the guilty nation. Those addressed were not, as some commentators suggest, the polluted children of the adulteress, since the negative was dropped and the relationship resumed. They were Jehovah's people on whom He had compassion.

Then he bluntly stated that their mother was not his wife and that he was not her husband. C. H. Gordon says that the phrase he used was the Hebrew equivalent of the Akkadian divorce formula. While it is true that Hosea may have put away Gomer, the verses which follow make it clear that the Divine purpose for Israel was not divorce but reconciliation. God had no intention of permanently casting off His people. He might punish them for their wrongdoing, but His compassion never failed and His purpose was immutable. But she was not a wife to Him, and He could not stand as a husband to her in her existing state.

Consequently He entreated that she would put away her harlotry from her face and her adultery from between her breasts. A harlot was identifiable by the veil with which she covered her face (Gen. 38 : 14). Even today a prostitute is often recognisable by her brazen shamelessness: her face reveals her character. The amulets and charms and other jewellery with which the unchaste woman bedecked herself were intended to allure the unwary, who might be seduced by the bosom of the strange woman (Prov. 5 : 19, 20). Her finery was to be swept away if there was to be reconciliation; the shameless effrontery was to be wiped from her face; the illicit love which bruised her breasts (Ezek. 23 : 8) was to be rejected.

The words could not be restricted to Gomer: her conduct was symbolical of Israel's behaviour. The nation's adultery was with Baalim. The people might persuade themselves that they were worshipping Jehovah through the ritual of the

Canaanite religion, but God relentlessly tore away the pretence and revealed their religion for what it was—the spiritual adultery of a nation espoused to Him. Although He appeared as a plaintiff in a legal scene, it was not to indulge in litigation for the putting away of the guilty one. His plea that she should strip herself of her embellishments (and the description given may have been a pejorative reference to the items worn by the devotees of the cult—see verse 13), was that she might thereby forswear her previous attitude and turn in repentance to Him. He sought reconciliation.

If the nation declined to amend its ways, there was no alternative but discipline. The legal punishment for adultery was death (Lev. 20 : 10), but it was the custom in some Middle Eastern nations to strip the woman of her clothes (Ezek. 16 : 39) and then to expel her from home. The Nuzi Tablets, for example, quote one case, "If Wishirur goes to another husband and lives with him, my sons shall strip off the clothes of my wife and they shall drive her out of my house." This was the utmost indignity. Jehovah declared that, if there was no reformation, He would strip His guilty wife naked. This was metaphorical, of course. A husband's duty was to clothe his wife and Jehovah had provided the wool and flax of the land, but now Israel was to be deprived of these gifts.

God was married to the land as well as to the nation and the language He employed related to both. The conditions of both were to revert to those applicable when they first became the holy land and the people of God. The remainder of verse 3, however, had its primary application to the land. Drought would dry up the land and leave it barren and parched, with nothing to slake its thirst. The harvest would fail and the futility of the worship of Baal (the god of rain) would become apparent. The land would lose its fertility and the people would be destitute.

CHILDREN OF ADULTERY

And I will not have compassion on her children, for they

31

are the children of harlotry. For their mother has played the harlot. She who conceived them has acted shamefully: for she said, I will go after my lovers, who give me my bread and my water, my wool and my flax, my oil and my drink (Hos. 2 : 4, 5).

In verse 2 the children had been summoned to take part in the case against the erring wife, but now they themselves were brought under review. Jehovah declared that He would not have compassion on them because they were the children of fornication. They were the offspring of a faithless mother and were regarded as sharing her guilt. The sins of the parent were to be visited on the children. Because of Israel's association with Baal, the Israelites were deemed to be children of that union and, therefore, to have no relationship to Jehovah. They were metaphorically the result of an adulterous union. Justifiably He declared that He would have no compassion on them; they were not His and had no claim upon Him. A new generation had grown up to whom the worship of Baal was the accepted religion and to whom Jehovah was little more than a name. In consequence, it was not merely the nation as a corporate body that was to suffer. Every member of the kingdom was to pay the penalty.

Espoused to Jehovah, Israel had deliberately and wilfully adopted the cult of Baalism. Jehovah accordingly accused the nation plainly of adultery. They had been false to Him and had acted shamefully. He had bestowed upon them every material benefit which they enjoyed. But when they had entered Canaan, the people had discovered the general belief that the fruitfulness of the land depended upon the union of Baal and the land, and had foolishly accepted the superstitions of the heathen.

God declared that the nation was more reprehensible than the common prostitute, who waited for customers to come to her. Israel eagerly pursued her lovers: she unhestitatingly went after the Canaanite deities of the fertility cult, on the assumption that from them she would receive all she needed—

32

bread, water, wool, flax, oil and wine. The Canaanites believed that these were the gifts of the Baalim, and Israel put her trust in the same deities. Her attitude was no different from the mercenariness of the prostitute. Yet she had known the beneficent hand of God and her experience should have taught her that the products of the land were His gift alone.

It seems amazing that a people who had experienced so much of God's deliverance and protection and constant provision could ever have declined in such a way. Yet the same possibilities exist today. It is still the same God who provides for His people, but how many put their confidence in other things, and give up their trust in Him for what seems more logical and—from a human point of view—more reliable. The blunt terms used by the Almighty centuries ago are still applicable.

HEDGED IN

Therefore, behold, I will hedge up her way with thorns, and make a wall against her so that she shall not find her paths (Hos. 2 : 6).

God refused to give up His erring people. If the nation eagerly sought the Baalim, He determined to put every possible obstacle in her way. If she pursued her illicit lovers, He would make it difficult for her to find them. He declared that He would surround her way with a hedge of thorns and build a wall against her which would prevent her discovering the path. She should be treated as a wayward animal to be penned in to prevent it wandering away. The loss of the products of the field was to be accompanied by the infliction of suffering. The nation had accepted the Baalim, but would now be cut off from the false deities by an impenetrable hedge.

LOST PARAMOURS

And she shall pursue her lovers, but shall not overtake them; and she shall seek them, but shall not find them. Then shall she say, I will go and return to my first husband; for then was better with me than now (Hos. 2 : 7).

C

The guilty nation was described as avidly and determinedly pursuing her paramours. With no consciousness of her need of Jehovah, Israel was concerned only with the Baalim. But God declared figuratively that she would be unable to overtake them: she might eagerly seek them but would not find them. The prosperity which the nation thought had been due to the providence of Baal had disappeared. Sacrifices, prayers, ritual and ceremony had lost their imagined efficacy: Baal gave no answer. The land was no longer fruitful and, refusing to acknowledge that Jehovah was the bestower of all the good gifts of life, Israel sought still more desperately for Baal. If he supplied the needs of their Canaanite neighbours, he must be able to supply theirs too. But Baal gave no answer to their petitions.

Finally the nation declared that she would return to her first husband (i.e. Jehovah) for she was better off then. There was no penitence or contrition. She thought ruefully of the benefits once enjoyed and decided that, if these could be renewed by a return to Jehovah, it was the only sensible course to take. The implication of Hosea's description was clear. The people had not concluded that the Baal worship was wrong or that the gifts of the land were not his. There was no repudiation of the false deity or of the idolatrous system. They merely recollected that greater prosperity had been enjoyed initially, and they were prepared to turn to Jehovah in the hope that the days of blessing would return once more. This was not repentance.

THE SOURCE OF BLESSING

She did not know that it was I who gave her corn and new wine and oil, and who lavished upon her silver and gold, which they used for Baal. Therefore I will return and will take back my corn in its time, and my new wine in its season, and will recover my wool and my flax, which were to cover her nakedness (Hos. 2 : 8, 9).

The essence of the Baalism, which was the indigenous

34

religion of Canaan, was that through the relation of the god with the land, the blessings of crops and general productivity were bestowed. The land was Baal's wife, whom he fertilised by rain. To induce his metaphorical intercourse with the land, the sexual rites, the *hieros gamos,* were celebrated by the god's servants and his followers. The local Baalim were merely representations of the deity with authority in particular localities, but similar rites were deemed necessary to secure their co-operation. The people of Israel had accepted the teachings of the cult unreservedly and had adopted the licentious practices of their neighbours. But it had been completely ineffective: the fertility, for which they hoped, was not forthcoming. They did not know, declared Jehovah, that He was the source of their material prosperity: it was He who gave them the corn, wine and oil they enjoyed. Instead of recognising Him as their Benefactor, they turned to the powerless gods of the heathen.

"She did not know." There was a depth of pathos in the words. After all the experiences of Jehovah's goodness and of His saving power, *they did not know.* That they should ever credit the gifts of the earth to a pagan deity after all they had received from God, seemed wellnigh incredible. But *they did not know.* That has always been true of some. They have been recipients of the mercy and compassion of the Almighty; they have been blessed with untold benefits; they have been guarded and protected from harm and danger; an eye has watched over them in every vicissitude of life. Yet they have been blind to the providential dealings of God. *They did not know* that it was from Him that every good was derived.

Israel's failure was even greater. The fruits of commerce, like the fruits of the field, were due to Divine goodness. They had prospered and had heaped together silver and gold. The Black Obelisk of Shalmaneser II refers to the many vessels of silver and gold paid to the Assyrians as tribute by Jehu. But Jehovah declared that they had used the silver and gold, which He had given them, for the service of Baal. The reference may have been to the overlaying with gold and silver of the images of Baal, or it may have been to the golden calves at Bethel, Dan and elsewhere. The insult was all the greater because they had lavished the gifts of God upon the false idol and the polluting cult of the false god.

For their blindness and for the sheer impertinence of their behaviour, Jehovah announced His intention of taking back again the gifts of His hand—the corn, wine, wool and flax. Why should He subsidise their idolatry? He had fulfilled His responsibility as the husband of land and nation: He had fed and clothed people and land. Now, however, He disclaimed His responsibility to provide for His unfaithful wife and stated that He was going to withdraw His gifts and leave her naked to her shame. The harvest would fail and they would be hungry and destitute. Vines and orchards would be fruitless and the wine of joy would be denied the people. Their commercial activities would prove unsuccessful and leave them in ignominious penury. Jehovah was not One with whom to trifle.

In a world which refuses to recognise God, the threat has still its relevance. "Every good and perfect gift," said James, "is from above and comes down from the Father of lights" (Jas. 1 : 17). Refusal to recognise Him as the source and the attribution of the blessings to our own effort or that of others may still result in our being deprived of what we value.

THE DISGRACED WIFE

Now I will disclose her lewdness in the sight of her lovers, and no one shall rescue her from my hand (Hos. 2 : 10).

Still using the symbolism of the unfaithful wife, stripped of the clothing provided by her husband and left naked in her shame, Jehovah stated that He would disclose her lewdness or shame (LXX, renders "impurity") to the eyes of her lovers. Exposed to the public gaze, her shame would revolt her paramours and they would turn away from her in abhorrence. Unable to provide her with the protection and covering which she had sought from them, their ineffectiveness and the futility of their worship would be apparent.

Jehovah was the God of nature. If He denied Israel the fruits of the earth and the material benefits she craved, no other power could supply them. The Baalim were impotent to help and the devotion paid to them by the guilty people was now exposed as misdirected and wasted. No one could help if Jehovah decided to inflict chastisement; He was supreme. The utter folly of Israel's attitude was evident.

JUDGMENT FALLS

I will also put an end to all her mirth, her feast days, her new moons, her sabbaths and all her appointed seasons. And I will lay waste her vines and her fig-trees, of which she said, These are my gifts which my lovers have given me. I will make them a forest and the beasts of the field shall devour them. And I will punish her for the days of Baalim, when she burned incense to them, and she decked herself with her earrings and her jewels, and she went after her lovers, and forgot me, says Jehovah (Hos. 2 : 11–13).

The relationship of Israel with Jehovah was marked by the celebration of appointed religious festivals and observances, which were times of rejoicing and happiness. Indeed, the word *hag*, used of the three annual pilgrimage festivals, is derived from a root meaning "to dance". Divine judgment was now to put an end to all this joyousness or, as G. A. Smith terms it, "joyaunce". Every sabbath day and at every new moon, certain offerings and libations were to be presented (Num. 28 : 9–15). Three times a year—at the feasts of unleavened bread, harvest, and ingathering—the people were required to appear before God (Ex. 23 : 14–17), but the religious calendar also contained other feast days and appointed seasons. These occasions of communion with the Eternal had been degraded to national holidays and occasions for social gatherings and merrymaking. The appointed festivals did not cease when the northern kingdom split off from the south, but they were now being transformed into festive occasions for the practice of the fertility cult. They were no longer Jehovah's festivals and He described them as Israel's ("*her* mirth, *her* feast days, *her* new moons, *her* sabbaths and all *her* appointed seasons").

She had boasted of the blessings which had accrued to her in consequence of the fertility rites in which she indulged. The fruits of the land, the textiles which had been manufactured, the profits made in trading, had all been attributed to the blessing of Baal. These were, she claimed, the gifts presented to her by her Baalim paramours, the fees she had received as a prostitute. But these had, in fact, been the gift of Jehovah. In stern justice He declared that He would destroy vineyard and orchard. If they were the gift of Baalim, He would demonstrate the total inability of the Baalim to preserve them.

Therefore, He would convert the fruitful field into a jungle (Isa. 5 : 6) and the wild beasts would devour both vine and fig. A depopulated country would naturally be overrun and devastated by the wild beasts, but the prophecy was probably anticipating also the ravages of the Assyrian enemy in a future day.

If Israel had neglected or degraded the festivals of Jehovah, she had meticulously observed the festal days of Baal. She had burned incense to the false deities and had decked herself with all her finery and jewellery on these holy days. She had donned earrings, nose rings and other jewels, the ornaments which, according to one writer, "had cultic significance of symbolic function". The adornment was not for spiritual reasons, but rather in order to attract her paramours. Although the language was metaphorical, there was also a tacit reference to the sexual practices associated with the cult.

The husband of Hosea's day had an authority over his wife and, in certain circumstances, he would feel free to punish her for wrongdoing. Israel had forgotten Jehovah and had followed the Baalim, and God justifiably declared that he would punish her for her worship of Baalim and for her conduct in serving these false deities.

HOPE FOR THE GUILTY
Therefore, behold, I will allure her and bring her into the

38

wilderness and speak tenderly to her. And there I will give her her vineyards, and the valley of Achor for a door of hope: there shall she respond, as in the days of her youth, as in the day when she came up out of the land of Egypt (Hos. 2 : 14, 15).

Having stripped the unfaithful wife of all the benefits she claimed to have received from her lovers and having disrupted her pursuit of them, the Eternal lover sought means of reconciling her to Himself. The material benefits allegedly derived from Baal had been denied to Israel, her attempts to indulge in the licentious practices of the cult had been hindered, and she had been left in a state of complete frustration and desolation.

Now Jehovah declared that He would coax or persuade her and bring her into the wilderness and there speak to her heart (*c.f.*, Ezek. 20 : 35). The word translated "allure" by the A.V. has rather the sense of appealing irresistibly, constraining to the extent of overwhelming all resistance: it was used of the forcible seduction of a virgin (Ex. 22 : 16). The love of Jehovah would completely overwhelm Israel as He wooed her again for Himself.

He would speak to her heart (Isa. 40 : 2) or, as G. A. Smith renders it, "speak home to her heart." He says (*op cit.*, p. 247) that it "is a forcible expression, like the German *an das Herz*, or the sweet Scottish *it cam' up roond my heart*, and was used in Israel as from man to woman when he won her." In the coming exile, He would teach her afresh His love and induce her dependence upon Him as He did after her exodus from Egypt. She could never reform herself unaided and His discipline of her was intended to be educational: it was for the purpose of bringing her back to Himself.

If Israel's land was in punishment to be handed over to the Assyrians, it was not for their permanent possession. It was the Divine intention to restore her vineyards to her. In the valley of Achor, the valley leading up from Jericho into the promised land, trouble had befallen Israel because of the covetousness of Achan. They had been routed at Ai and not until sin had been judged could they continue their course (Josh. 7). But the vale of trouble, where Achan and his family had been put to death, was now to be transformed for the people. It was the route into the land: it was to become for Israel a door of hope. There was possibly the reminder that sin must be confessed and put away if blessing was to result.

Then would Israel respond (or sing) as in the days of her youth, declared Jehovah. The experiences of the exodus from Egypt would be renewed and the joy of that day be repeated (Ex. 15 : 1). The Divine purposes for the failing people had not been abrogated; nothing could frustrate God's will. The exile must come as a judicial punishment, but already He disclosed that restoration and reconciliation must follow. The promise has only partially been fulfilled, so that plainly a more complete fulfilment must be achieved in the future. Israel will once more occupy her own land and experience the blessing of Jehovah.

NO MORE BAAL

And it shall be at that day, says Jehovah, that you will call me Ishi and will no more call me Baali. For I will take away the names of Baalim out of her mouth, and they shall be mentioned by name no more (Hos. 2 : 16, 17).

In verses 16, 18 and 21 the prophecy referred to "that day". It is clear that the reference was not merely to the period of the return from exile—when, in any case, comparatively few returned—but to a future date of which that was only a foretaste. The complete fulfilment of God's plan for Israel has not yet been seen and its implementation awaits the days of Messiah.

Israel had named Him Baal, i.e. lord or master, but this name had assumed a pagan connotation, and the designation of Jehovah by this term encouraged the tendency to the syncretism of Jehovah and Baal. Moreover, the word Baal carried the implication of ownership and tacitly emphasised the rights of the husband over the wife. Instead of Baal, Israel was to use the name Ishi, i.e., my husband, which was a much more intimate and personal term. She would then realise the depth of love in her Maker-Husband and, in complete devotion, surrender herself to Him. Never again would she use the term Baal of Him. Henceforth it would be Ishi.

Indeed the name was to be completely excised. Israel had become completely entangled in the cult of Baalim, but God promised that He would remove the names of the Baalim from her mouth. Never again would she be able to utter them. They could never be mentioned by name again. This clearly implied that all thought of the polluting cult would be expunged from the people's memory. It would be a thing of the past, with no further hold over them. When God delivers, the work is complete. He frees from the very power of the devilish influences which once dominated the life. He sets the captive free.

JEHOVAH'S COVENANT

And in that day I will make a covenant for you with the beasts of the field and with the fowls of heaven and with the creeping things of the ground. And I will break the bow and the sword and the battle out of the land, and will make you lie down in safety (Hos. 2 : 18).

In the day of blessing, to which He had already referred, Jehovah declared that He would make a covenant with beasts, birds and reptiles: the terms of the covenant were not detailed, but presumably the intention was to impose a prohibition upon them, forbidding them to do harm to the people of Israel. The wild beasts were to lose their ferocity and be deprived of their enmity to man: this, of course, was the picture painted by the contemporary prophet Isaiah (Isa. 11 : 6–9) in a clear reference to the Messianic era.

The phraseology used for the making of the covenant was that employed for the "cutting" or "confirming" of a treaty, when both parties passed between the pieces of animals, reciting the terms of the treaty and calling down imprecations upon themselves for any breach thereof for which they might become responsible. Such a treaty was completely binding on the parties thereto. The concept of a covenant with all living creatures was perhaps somewhat picturesque; what was envisioned was presumably an ordinance or command imposed upon them by God.

All military equipment was also to be banished from the land and an end put to all conflict or warfare in Israel. Referring to the same period, Isaiah predicted that military weapons would be converted into agricultural implements and that war would be abolished (Isa. 2 : 4). As a result, the people would lie down in safety; fear would never again grip their hearts (cf. Lev. 26 : 6). There is no doubt that the prophet anticipated the peaceful reign of the Messiah for the glorious millennial age and was adding his confirmation to the assurances given by so many of the prophets.

REMARRIAGE

And I will betroth you to me for ever. I will betroth you to me in righteousness, in justice, in loving kindness and in compassion. I will betroth you to me in faithfulness: and you shall know Jehovah (Hos. 2 : 19, 20).

According to Lehrman (*op. cit.,* p. 11), verses 19 and 20 "are recited when the phylacteries are donned. They carry the Jew back to the revelation on Sinai when God effected a spiritual marriage with Israel, with the Torah as dowry. The threefold repetition of 'I will betroth you' denotes affection and permanence."

Israel had been portrayed as the unfaithful wife of Jehovah, but now He declared His intention of betrothing her to Himself again. Betrothal in Old Testament days was of greater importance and was more binding than the formal engagement of western society. It was virtually equivalent to marriage itself. A betrothed woman was regarded as a married one (Deut. 20 : 7; 22 : 23–27). The word used (*aras*) appears eleven times in the Old Testament. It included even the payment of the bride-price (*mohar*).

This second betrothal of Israel was to be permanent and the bond would be indissoluble; nothing would mar the harmony of the union or create any difference between Jehovah and His people. The price of the bride had been settled and the betrothal would be accompanied by the payment of the price: it was to be righteousness, justice, lovingkindness, compassion (or tender mercies) and faithfulness. These were attributes of Jehovah Himself and a guarantee, therefore, of the permanence of the union.

The marriage gift to the bride was to be the knowledge of Jehovah. Once she had forgotten Him and there was no knowledge of God in the land. Now the character of the Eternal was to be revealed to the nation in all its magnitude and wonder, and in the realisation of His glory, majesty and sufficiency, she would never turn her eyes elsewhere. This would be no academic or intellectual knowledge, but a spiritual understanding and appreciation of the worth of the Beloved. Today the revelation of God has been made in Christ: the soul gazes upon Him and is lost in wonder and amazement at the unveiling of the character and being of God.

UNIVERSAL RESPONSE

In that day, I will answer, says Jehovah. I will answer the heavens and they shall answer the earth; and the earth shall answer the corn and the new wine and the oil; and they shall answer Jezreel. And I will sow her for myself in the land; and I will have mercy on Lo-ruhamah; and I will say to Lo-ammi, You are my people; and they shall say, My God (Hos. 2 : 21–23).

In judgment the land had suffered drought; the corn, wine and oil had failed; the wool and flax had been lost. In the millennial age, to which the prophecy now referred, all would be completely changed. Jehovah would no longer be deaf to the cries of His people, but would answer their petitions with blessing. If the relationship with Jehovah was restored, then

43

the fruitfulness of the land would be an indication of this reconciliation, since all blessing originated in Him. Hosea portrayed the heavens as crying to God that they might be allowed to supply the earth with the rain to ensure its fertility; and he saw the earth sighing for the rains of heaven which had been so long withheld.

As T. K. Cheyne (*Hosea*, p. 56) says, "It is a beautiful picture of harmony between the physical and the spiritual spheres,. Jezreel (i.e. Israel) asks its plants to germinate; they call upon the earth for its juices; the earth beseeches heaven for rain; heaven supplicates for the divine word which opens the stores; and Jehovah responds in faithful love." By inference, the fruits of the earth are produced abundantly in consequence of the chain of prayer which links earth to the footstool of God.

Somewhat curiously the prophecy reverted to the children of Gomer. The sinister connotation given to Jezreel in Hos. 1 disappeared and the usual significance of the word appeared. In the fruitful valley of Jezreel (meaning "God sows"), God announced that He would sow Israel to Himself, implying that she would now be fruitful to Him.

Lo-ruhamah (whose name meant "no pity or compassion") representing the nation upon whom Jehovah could not have compassion because of her apostasy and spiritual adultery, was now to experience the compassion of Jehovah. Israel once more would know His mercy and grace. No longer Loruhamah, their name would be Ruhamah.

Similarly with the youngest child. As a figure of his people, the boy was named Lo-ammi (i.e. "not my people"), but Jehovah now announced that He would address Israel as Ammi (i.e. "My people"). The shadows of the past had been dispersed. Mercy and forgiveness surmounted every barrier. And in reply to the grace of Jehovah, the people would respond in adoring worship with the cry, "My God". That day has not yet come, but the indications are that the end of the present age is imminent, and that the dawn of Israel's day cannot, therefore, be far distant.

CHAPTER 4

The Erring Wife

THERE has been considerable controversy regarding the identity of the woman described in Hosea 3. The majority of expositors take the view that this chapter was still concerned with the prophet's wife, Gomer: the narrative in chapter 1, on this basis, related to the marriage of Hosea in good faith to his bride who, at that time, had not fallen into sin, although she may have had evil propensities. After her infidelity and expulsion from home, the prophet sought her out and brought her back and, after disciplining her, resumed his marital relationship with her. This seems the most logical interpretation. Some commentators, however, argue that chapters 1 and 3 both refer to the same happening and not to two stages in the history of Gomer. Others place the events of chapter 3 before those in chapter 1 and claim that Hosea purchased a woman of loose morals, disciplined her and, assuming that he had effected a reformation in her, married her, only to discover that she was still unfaithful.

A not insignificant body of opinion, on the other hand, supports the view that the chapters refer to two different women. On the basis of this interpretation, chapter 1 recounted the story of Hosea's marriage to a woman who, he subsequently discovered, was sexually promiscuous, whereas chapter 3 narrated a symbolic action concerning a female slave and concubine. On the whole, it seems more logical to regard the story as stages in the prophet's conjugal experiences. Since the typological application is to Israel, the significance would be partly lost and certainly confused if two women were involved.

UNDYING LOVE

Then said Jehovah to me, Go again, love a woman who is beloved of a paramour and is an adulteress, even as Jehovah loves the people of Israel, who turn to other gods and love raisin cakes. So I bought her for fifteen shekels of silver and a homer of barley and a lethech of barley (Hos. 3 : 1, 2).

In the previous chapter the prophey had predicted the ultimate restoration of Israel and her blessing during the millennial reign of Messiah. Jehovah had set the example of pardon and forgiveness and of a re-betrothal in love and compassion. It was necessary for the lesson to be taught before Hosea understood the Divine purpose for himself. In his personal sorrow he had entered into the feelings of God: because of his own grief he could sympathise with God's. But now, conversely, Jehovah had intimated His intention of reconciling Israel to Himself and of restoring her to favour. The example was for Hosea to appreciate and understand. If Jehovah could forgive and restore, should not His servant follow the same course?

That this was the Divine will was made perfectly clear. Hosea had set his love on Gomer when he deemed her a spotless bride, but his love had obviously not waned, even after her infidelity and departure from him. The God of mercy accordingly—and in perfect consistency with His own purpose in a wider field—bade him go once more and show his love to his shameless wife, although she was described deprecatingly, not as a *wife* but merely as a *woman*. Gomer had displayed no sign of contrition or of any desire to return. When Hosea found her, her sin was blatant: she was beloved of a paramour and flagrantly adulterous. How could anyone love a wretch so devoid of honour or self-respect?

Yet Jehovah pointed to His own example. Israel was equally culpable, but He loved the nation and destined its

46

blessing. Hosea was told that his love should follow the pattern of God's: it was to be "even as Jehovah loves the people of Israel". They were no more deserving an object. They turned the face to other gods and loved cakes of grapes or raisins, said the Divine Speaker. Jehovah, seeking His people, had found them occupied with the Baalim and, at the autumn festival, presenting to the false deities cakes of dried grapes or raisins, a luxury which they shared with the priests. They had no desire for Jehovah and were obsessed with their sensual devotion to Baal. Nevertheless He loved them and intended their good. If this was possible for the Eternal, it was not impossible for the prophet.

Hosea does not seem to have hesitated. Gomer had sold herself into slavery. Unquestioning, the prophet bought back the woman he loved. The state of degradation to which she had sunk was revealed by the price he paid to her owner. The price of a slave was thirty shekels (Exod. 21 : 32). This Hosea paid, half in silver and half in kind. One and a half homers of barley (the cheapest of the grains) made up the price. (The word *lethech*, used in the passage, does not appear elsewhere in the Old Testament, but has been generally regarded as the equivalent of half a homer. G. A. Smith suggests that the third item was a lethech of wine, but there is nothing to support this.) The offer of barley to make up the price marked even morely clearly the depressed condition of the woman, for barley was despised as food.

Under the law a divorced wife who had lived with another man could not return to her former husband (Deut. 24 : 4) and this was confirmed centuries later (Jer. 3 : 1). As for Israel, so for Gomer, however, grace was greater than law, and mercy went farther than legal requirements.

DISCIPLINE

And I said to her, You shall abide with me many days. You shall not play the harlot, and you shall not be for any other man. So will I also be towards you (Hos. 3 : 3).

Hosea had redeemed his wife from a state of concubinage, but she had demonstrated no change of heart or inclination. It was essential, therefore, to prove her dependability if he was to restore her to favour. All that had happened so far was that he had cut short her immoral course and had prevented her indulging in further licentiousness. Justifiably he told her that she was to live in quiet seclusion in his home for a considerable period (cf. Deut. 21 : 13), presumably until he was satisfied with her conduct.

She was to be prevented from engaging in prostitution and debarred from sexual intercourse with any other man. Hosea guaranteed furthermore that he himself would abstain from relations with any other woman and, until the period of exemplary detention ended, he would not resume conjugal relations with his wife. It was not an unreasonable procedure in the light of her previous conduct and was directed at restricting her desires and affections for anyone save her husband. The course adopted by the prophet, obviously under Divine direction, was intended additionally as an illustration of the manner in which God intended dealing with Israel.

DAYS OF DEPRIVATION

For the people of Israel shall abide many days without a king and without a prince, and without a sacrifice and without a pillar, and without an ephod and without teraphim (Hos. 3 : 4).

The expressions used by the prophet, in intimating the restrictions he proposed placing upon his wife, were reiterated in Jehovah's words to Israel. They were to abide in seclusion for many days, i.e. for a considerable period. During that time, they would be deprived of all that they normally valued, so that they might be forced to a realisation of the complete sufficiency of Jehovah and the ineffectiveness of all else. The civil and religious institutions, which had seemed of such outstanding importance, were taken away and the people left without support. It is evident that the reference is to the period of exile, when Israel was denied all her former privileges and was taught in captivity what she had lost because of her sin. Like adulterous Gomer, the spiritually unfaithful Israel was to have time to meditate upon the past, upon her sins and infidelity, upon the despite done to God, and upon all the blessings she had sacrificed to her transient enjoyment of the things of Baal.

During the period of solitariness, Israel was to be deprived of king and prince. The entire administration would collapse. For most nations the king represented the whole of the institutions: he sustained the fabric of the whole nation. The elders and functionaries, both civil and military, derived their authority from the king. If king and princes, leaders and magistrates and the whole royal and judicial system disappeared, the country would be thrown into a state of chaos. The nation would virtually be defunct. But, in the Assyrian captivity, of course, everything was lost, and the people were left leaderless and disorganised.

Jehovah intended to chastise idolatrous Israel still further by depriving the nation of its religious institutions. In exile the people would be unable to present the usual sacrifices and offerings to Jehovah. They had presented their offerings to Baal and had ignored Jehovah. Now they would lose the opportunity of sacrificing to any god. The spiritual and psychological relief resulting from the presenting of sin and trespass offerings would be denied to them. The assurance of communion with God, which came from the peace offerings and burnt offerings would no longer be theirs. There would be no sacrifice.

In the Canaanite religion, every holy place or shrine was marked by an upright stone or pillar (*mazzebah*), which was regarded as a symbol of the male deity and in which, in some cases, he was deemed to reside. Such pillars were forbidden by the law (Deut. 16 : 32), but, in the northern kingdom, they were initially treated as symbols of Jehovah. In some instances, they were smeared with the fat or blood of the sacrifices (cf. Gen. 28 : 18). They were denounced as idolatrous

D

(1 Kings 14 : 23; 2 Kings 17 : 10). Even these *mazzeboth*, in which the people had trusted, were to be taken from them: they were left with nothing in exile.

The people were additionally to be deprived of an ephod. There is some difference of opinion as to the character of the ephod. That constructed by Gideon at Ophrah, to which Israel resorted, seems to have been an image or idol (Jud. 8 : 27). The one made by Micah of Mount Ephraim also seems to have been an idol (Jud. 17 : 5; 18 : 14, 17–20, 24). The ephod referred to by Ahimelech, when referring to the hiding place of Goliath's sword, may also have been an image of some kind (1 Sam. 21 : 9; see also 1 Sam. 23 : 6, 9; 30 : 7). The word was normally used, however, with reference to the richly embroidered and coloured garment worn by the high priest over which was the jewelled breastplate, containing the Urim and Thummim (Exod. 28 : 6–14). By enquiry of the high priest and the lights and shadows upon these mysterious stones, the will of God was ascertained. During the nation's exile, the ephod would no longer be available. Not only would there be no high priest, but no provision for discovering the mind of God.

Finally, there would be no teraphim. Like the *Penates* of the Romans, the teraphim were small images, often of ancestors, which were regarded as the source of prosperity but also as oracular deities from whom enquiry might be made. Those used by Michal to represent her husband, David, must have been somewhat larger (1 Sam. 19 : 13). They were among other forms of necromancy and divination which Josiah put away in his day (2 Kings 23 : 24). There is no confirmation that teraphim were used in the Canaanite religion, but they had certainly been used by Israel through the centuries. Even these idolatrous objects were now taken from them.

They were left without any of the religious helps they had so often employed and without any of the institutions in which they had trusted, either true or false. Like Gomer, they were left to meditate on their ways, to realise their folly, to see their spiritual adultery in its true light, and to come to their senses. It must be inferred that Gomer's discipline brought her to a state of quiet submission and surrender to her husband, and possibly to a renewal of devotion to him. This was Jehovah's purpose for Israel and this too was achieved.

Afterwards shall the people of Israel return and seek Jehovah their Elohim, and David their king; and shall be in awe of Jehovah and his goodness in the latter days (Hos. 3 : 5).

When the time of discipline was ended, the prophecy declared that Israel would return and seek Jehovah their God. It can scarcely be claimed that this prediction has been fulfilled, but the prophecy linked the fulfilment with "the latter days", which, Kimchi argued, always referred to the days of Messiah. When He returns to establish His theocratic rule upon earth, Israel will recognise Him and turn to Him. Despite the number of Jews who have returned to their own land today, there has been no national religious revival and no widespread turning to God. But in that day, when Messiah takes the reins of government into His hands, Israel will flock to Jehovah and recognise Him once more as their God.

The prophet declared, moreover, that they would return to seek "David their king". In Hosea's days, the royal power was constantly changing through murder and assassination. There was no stability or security. But there is One to come who will govern with a rod of iron and who will tolerate no rebellion or opposition. David was regarded as the prototype of perfect kingship (Ezek. 34 : 23; 37 : 24), and the Targum of Jonathan identifies him here with the King Messiah. The reference was, of course, to the Davidic dynasty and not to David personally. The ruler referred to would be one from David's line, the Lord Jesus Christ.

The people then would render Jehovah the worshipful fear or awe due to Him—that fear which is the beginning of wisdom (Prov. 1 : 7). Israel had sought the Baalim for the pros-

51

perity they allegedly bestowed, ignoring the fact that the good gifts they craved were bestowed by Jehovah. Now they would find the desired "goodness"—the grain, oil, wine, flax and wool—in Jehovah and give to Him the worship of fear.

If that glorious day has not yet come, it cannot long be postponed. The stage is set, the actors are in the wings, and it seems probable that the drama will soon commence. When it does, Israel will suffer as never before, but ultimately the clouds will disperse at the advent of the King of kings and Lord of lords. Every desire then will be satisfied and the people, who have suffered so much and so long, will be restored to Divine favour.

CHAPTER 5

The Nation's Character

FROM the portrayal of millennial blessing and prosperity, Hosea reverted to the conditions of his own period. Sitting as judge, Jehovah summoned Israel to hear Him also as plaintiff. He was about to deliver His charge against His people. It has been suggested that the long reign of Jeroboam II had finished and that the eventual anarchy which wrecked the country had begun with the reign of Menahem.

JEHOVAH'S CONTROVERSY

Hear the word of Jehovah, you people of Israel. For Jehovah has a controversy with the inhabitants of the land. There is no steadfastness, nor lovingkindness, nor knowledge of Elohim in the land. By swearing, and lying, and murder and theft and adultery, they break all bounds, and blood mingles with blood (Hos. 4 : 1, 2).

The story of Hosea and Gomer sank into oblivion and did not recur again in the remainder of the book. It had served its purpose to illustrate the character of Israel and the way in which Jehovah intended to deal with her.

The people were now summoned to the legal court to hear the case to be presented against them. The arraignment was deliberately expressed in forensic terms. As J. L. Mays (*Hosea*, p. 62) writes, "Because the covenant was a relationship which had a content of legal requirements enforced by the punishment of curses, judicial process lent itself easily to the language in which the prophets spoke of covenant rupture between God and people."

In the opening accusation, Jehovah first detailed the people's sins of omission and commission. There were three major sins of omission and five of commission. There was no truth or steadfastness (possibly faithfulness), no lovingkindness and no knowledge of God in the land. The dependability of the one, whose word was reliable and who would be unshaken by any circumstances, was conspicuous by its absence: mutual trust had disappeared since good faith no longer existed. The steadfast love or unfailing devotion to Jehovah or to their fellows was a quality legitimately to be expected from the covenant nation, but it was missing.

But the basic deficiency, the cardinal sin of omission, was the absence of the knowledge of God. Little else mattered beside this. There was no appreciation of the character of God and no understanding of His ways and His purposes for man. His standards of behaviour and morality, His requirements of consistent conduct and relationships, His conditions of blessing—these meant nothing: they were not even realised. The knowledge of God, as one writer says, "involves uprightness of moral life, probity, both on an individual and social level. And it involves spirituality, i.e. an inward conviction of the reality of God." If these had failed, how could Israel boast of a relationship with Jehovah? They had virtually identified God with Nature, by whom the material needs of life were met. Religion had sunk to its lowest level.

Israel's sins of commission were equally blatant. The prophet set out their crimes in five verbal nouns—swearing, lying, killing, stealing and committing adultery. There could scarcely be a more complete breach of the law and, therefore, breach of the contract or covenant between Jehovah and His people.

The swearing was not so much the pronouncement of a malediction upon another, the uttering of a curse or imprecation upon an enemy, as the false swearing or perjury characteristic of the nation in Hosea's day (Exod. 20 : 16). It was not profanity so much as deceit and the bearing of false witness.

Lying was, of course, an equally deplorable offence. It affected the people in every sphere of life, but was particularly evident in the commercial field. Neither buyer nor seller could trust each other; there was the deception of fraudulent balances. They lied to the priest, to God, to the judge and to the merchant. How could God countenance the conduct of such people?

The decalogue had explicitly commanded that Israel should not kill (Exod. 20 : 13), but here was a nation in which murder was an accepted feature of the day. If anger rose against another, a man's hand was ready to strike, whether or not the ire was justifiable. Since mercy had vanished, revenge was only too prevalent. In no small scale, murder stained the land.

Where moral standards had disappeared, the recognition of others' rights also disappeared. As Amos so clearly indicated, justice was often perverted that the wealthy might secure their own ends and appropriate property which belonged to a poorer man. The expropriation was no other than plain theft. What was practised by those in authority was imitated by others on a smaller scale. The whole society was corrupt and selfish. If theft was pardonable in the upper classes, it was argued that it was permissible in other circles.

The religious rites, in which the people participated, countenanced prostitution and inevitably led eventually to widespread adultery. Morality no longer had any significance. The lust inspired by the religious practices consumed the whole being and immorality became general. The nation's outlook was coloured by the requirements of Baalism and the adultery of the shrine set the pattern for the infidelity of the home (Exod. 20 : 14).

Mays (*op. cit.*, p. 65) pertinently writes, "The proliferation of such deeds shows that the northern state had already sunk to the level of a chaotic society which has no recognisable relation to the divine law." The law had been deliberately broken and the curses which were to fall upon the transgressor had clearly been invoked.

The prophecy had its message for Israel centuries ago, but it is no less relevant today, for the sins of Hosea's day are the sins of the twentieth century. Dr. J. Zwemer says, in *The Immoral Revolution,* "Crime is rampant and increasing. Unrest is universal. Drug addiction is a national calamity in the U.S. The sex revolution is sweeping across the land. The seventh commandment has been torn to shreds. In many places, homosexuals are lauded and promoted. Pornography has become a religion, and prostitutes the priestesses of it . . . Society has reached the point where sin has become a science, and those who are its devotees would enforce it upon us." Dr. Billy Graham has said, "If God does not punish America, He should apologise to Sodom and Gomorrah," but there are few other countries which are not equally guilty.

The people broke all bounds, declared Jehovah. Like a turbulent river overflowing its banks, they burst all bounds of morality and righteousness by their bloody deeds and violent acts. Blood mingled with blood: murder had become commonplace. All restrictions were swept away in the onrush of iniquity; life was held lightly and no standards were regarded as binding. There could be only one result.

THE CONSEQUENCE

Therefore the land mourns and all who dwell in it languish, with the beasts of the field and the fowls of heaven; even the fish of the sea shall be taken away (Hos. 4 : 3).

The moral depravity of Israel had polluted the land and the Divine judgment upon the nation of necessity affected the inanimate creation as well. Among the punishments invoked by disobedience to the law were drought, locusts and the loss of flocks and herds (Deut. 28 : 24–42), and evidently these were to be inflicted upon Israel for her wrongdoing in Hosea's day. As a result, the land mourned for lack of rain and the destruction of the crops. It withered in despair. Tragedy came not only to the human beings but to the animals, birds and even fish. There was no food for cattle or sheep or for the birds of the air, and they languished and died because of the far-reaching catastrophe. No created thing escaped. Even the fish of the sea perished. It was impossible not to see the punitive hand of God in all these calamities.

PRIEST AND PROPHET

Let no man contend or reprove another; for your people are as they who contend with the priest. Therefore you shall stumble by day, and the prophet also shall stumble with you by night, and I will cut off your mother (Hos. 4 : 4, 5).

The land lay waste and it seems that recriminations were being hurled by one at another. This exercise was futile. It has been suggested that these words were uttered at one of the agricultural festivals at one of the national sanctuaries. The people were reproving and upbraiding one another and even accusing the prophet and the priest, attributing the conditions which were existing to the sin of one of those accused. This was a fruitless exercise since they were all culpable: their contumacy was obvious to all.

Horton (*op. cit.*, p. 28) renders verse 4, "Yet let no man strive with or blame the people: for the people only follow their priests, who have turned religion into ritual, and have neglected the instruction in the knowledge of God, which was their two functions."

The people were not the most to blame and should not indulge in idle criticism of each other. The basic culpability was the priest's. Ewald suggests that the significance is that the people "will not permit anyone, even a prophet, to contend with them, although they themselves do not scruple in the least to quarrel with everyone, even with the priest who would admonish them, in spite of the traditional reverence for his office." Jehovah's controversy was primarily with the priesthood.

The court hearing completed, the verdict on the priest was

57

about to be implemented. He would stumble in the day. If the priest stumbled in the clear light of day, the prophet would also stumble with him in the night. The prophets to whom Hosea referred were the official hierarchy, who adopted the role of prophet as a means of livelihood, and who were probably servants of the Canaanite cult. Both they and the priests would fall.

God declared, moreover, that He would destroy their mother, i.e., the stock from which they had sprung, not their literal mother. The reference was presumably to the whole of their clan and not to the entire Jewish race. The priests would suffer in the Assyrian invasion in the same way as anyone else.

NO KNOWLEDGE

My people are cut off for lack of knowledge. Because you have rejected knowledge, I reject you from being a priest to me. Since you have forgotten the law of your God (Elohim), I will also forget your children (Hos. 4 : 6).

Hosea considered the primary function of the priests to be the teaching of the people. Apart from their instruction there could be no knowledge of God. This mattered more than anything else. The function of the priest was to lead (Mal. 2 : 7) and they had failed in this fundamental duty. They had rejected the revelation of the Divine will and had failed to provide the guidance anticipated from them. It was not the fact that it was a schismatic priesthood that was condemned, but the criminal neglect of a vital responsibility.

Since they had rejected the knowledge of God, Jehovah declared that He rejected them as priests. The priesthood was hereditary but, since they had forgotten the *torah* entrusted to them by God, He would forget their children. In other words, the priesthood would come to an end; it would cease to function in Israel.

LEADERS IN INIQUITY

The more they increased, the more they sinned against me.

58

I will change their glory into shame. They feed on the sin of my people, and they lift up their soul to their iniquity (Hos. 4 : 7, 8).

The indictment of the priesthood was damning. The more they multiplied and grew in wealth and power, the greater became their failure. In their self-sufficiency they apostasised from God and sinned against Him. They lost sight completely of their spiritual responsibilities and call, and were motivated only by mercenary desires. Therefore, Jehovah declared that the glory and honour of their position should be transformed into shame and infamy. Cheyne takes the view that they had themselves changed their glory into infamy.

The priesthood had become a lucrative office during the reign of Jeroboam. When animals were brought for sacrifice, the officiating priest received a portion of the animal, so that he had a vested interest in the people's sin. "They feed on the sin of my people," declared Jehovah. The word translated *sin* could equally properly be translated *sin offering*, so that there may have been a literal significance as well as the metaphorical. The greater the sin or the more numerous the transgressions, the greater the revenue of the priests. Pusey (*op. cit.,* p. 50) considers that, because their priesthood was schismatic and was associated only with the false cult, "they upheld the sin whereby they lived and, that they might themselves be accounted priests of God, taught them to worship the calves as representatives of God." Hosea's reference, however, was to the trespass of the people rather than to the sinful system of worship.

Since the practice had grown up of exacting fees for the expiation of sins, it was obviously to the priests' advantage to encourage the people to live sinful lives. Instead of leading the people into a realisation of the holiness of God and the necessity for a pure and holy life, they not only made no attempt to stem the tide of iniquity, but actually encouraged it for their own avaricious ends. Their appetites were greedily lifted up at the thought of their profit from the people's iniquity. There could scarcely be any greater impropriety than that of the priest, whose duty was to nurture people in the faith, officially encouraging the transgressions of the sinner.

Is the church today less culpable? The law of God condemns homosexuality, for example (Lev. 18 : 22): yet so-called ministers of the gospel have established "gay" churches with a membership restricted to homosexuals. Anton La Vey's Church of Satan teaches the breaking of every command of the decalogue and the indulgence of every evil desire. If God condemned the insincere priesthood of a past day, will He be less tolerant in our day?

APOSTASY

And it shall be, like people, like priest. I will punish them for their ways and requite them for their deeds. For they shall eat but not be satisfied; they shall go a-whoring but shall not increase; because they have left off taking heed to Jehovah. Whoredom and wine and new wine take away the heart (Hos. 4 : 9–11).

The priests would not escape the consequences of their actions. Their official position would be no protection for them, and they would fare no better than the people. They had dishonoured God and He declared that He would punish them for their behaviour and requite them for their deeds. They may have deemed themselves secure, but the day of accounting was coming. There is always a full recompense with God, whether for good or evil.

The priests indulged their gluttony in devouring their portions of the sacrifices brought by the people to atone for their sins, but their greed was never satisfied. They should eat, said Jehovah, but remain hungry.

They participated in the *hieros gamos,* the ritual of sexual intercourse with the sacred prostitutes for the purpose of securing the fertility of the land. But the purpose of the ritual would be frustrated since the land lay under Jehovah's judgment, and the lust to which they gave rein produced no satisfaction. Moreover, in their shameful perversions, the reproductive faculty would cease to produce. The expected progeny would never come into existence. Their whoredom would be punished by childlessness. Retribution had fallen because they had left off taking heed to Jehovah. None can ignore God with impunity: sooner or later the recompense must come.

The impure rites of the nature worship, which priests had inculcated, had their permanent effect upon the people. The continual indulgence in licentiousness debauches not only the body but the mind. As a general principle, God stated that whoredom, wine and new wine destroy the spiritual understanding. The polluting ceremonies into which the priests led the worshippers inevitably destroyed respect for the marriage bond. The intoxication which accompanied the feasts robbed the individual of his powers of judgment and discernment. There was a price to pay for the worship of Baal.

BAAL'S HOLD

My people enquire at their stocks, and their staff declares to them. For a spirit of whoredoms has caused them to err and they have gone a-whoring from their God (Elohim). They sacrifice on the tops of the mountains, and burn incense on the hills, under oak, poplar and terebinth because their shade is good. Therefore your daughters commit whoredom and your spouses commit adultery. I will not punish your daughters when they play the whore, nor your spouses when they commit adultery. For they themselves go aside with consecrated prostitutes and they sacrifice with the prostitutes. A people that does not understand shall be dashed to the ground (Hos. 4 : 12–14).

The surrender of the people to the attractions of Baalism was complete. The pure worship of Jehovah, corrupted in the first instance by the introduction of Jeroboam's golden calves, had given way to the sensual rites of the Canaanite religion.

Instead of seeking guidance from Jehovah, Israel turned to "their stocks", a word usually rendered "tree" or "wood" in

61

the Old Testament, but translated "stocks" in Jer. 2 : 27; 3 : 9; 10 : 8. Hosea probably referred to the *asherah* or wooden pole erected by the side of the altar, but it is possible that the reference was to the wooden idol fashioned by the craftsman and overlaid with gold or silver (Isa. 40 : 19). So depraved were the people that they imagined that direction might be obtained from such an inanimate object.

They went farther, however, and resorted to the pagan arts of divination and particularly to rhabdomancy or divination by sticks. "Two rods were held upright," says C. F. Keil (*The Twelve Minor Prophets,* vol. 1, p. 80), "and then allowed to fall, while forms of incantation were being uttered; and the oracle was inferred from the way in which they fell" (*cf.* Ezek. 21 : 21). No longer did they rely upon Jehovah. The priests who should have taught them the truth of God had led them astray into the sensual nature-worship of the false cult.

It was a spirit of whoredom that had caused them to err, declared the prophet. Metaphorically, the idolatrous worship had led the nation into a spiritual adultery and a departure from God. But, in actual practice, the literal fornication and lewdness of the pagan cult were an indication of the overwhelming spirit of whoredom which had possessed them. They had, both literally and figuratively gone a-whoring from their God.

The demoralisation was evident from the whole of their religious practices. The old Canaanite shrines had been located in the "high places" on the tops of mountains and hills. Israel took them over and continued the ritual of the heathen fertility religion. They sacrificed to Baal in the high places and burned incense to Baal and Ashtoreth. In the shade of the oak, poplar and terebinth, they consumed the ceremonial meal. But the eating and drinking conduced to readiness for sexual intercourse with the *kedeshoth.* The idolatry and adultery were inextricably connected.

Moreover, the example set by the fathers in their adultery with the temple prostitutes inevitably had repercussions in the domestic sphere. The men could not engage in immorality and hope to retain the purity of the home. As a direct consequence of their conduct, their daughters and wives gave themselves up to fornication and adultery. (The word *kallah*, translated "spouse" in the A.V., could also be translated "bride" or daughter-in-law". A number of expositors adopt the last and some find an allusion to a practice—of which there is no record—of fathers having sexual intercourse with their prospective daughters-in-law before marriage to ensure the fertility of the marriage. But it is more logical to interpret the verse as applying to daughters and wives, who were those members of the household primarily affected by the father's example.) The temples provided male prostitutes for the female devotees, but Hosea was doubtless describing the general immorality of his day and not restricting it merely to the religious rites, although these were presumably included.

The attitude of the law to adultery was perfectly clear (Exod. 20 : 14; Deut. 22 : 22) and it might well have been expected that stringent action would have been demanded. On the contrary, God astonishingly declared that He would not punish the daughters and wives for their sexual promiscuity. Their guilt was unquestioned, even if it was limited to intercourse with male servants of the temple as part of the religious ritual. The reason for the apparent leniency was plainly stated : the men themselves went aside into the groves on the hillsides to commit adultery with the consecrated prostitutes and to sacrifice with them, i.e., to share the feast with them after the sacrifice (Exod. 32 : 6). The men dishonoured the marital relationship : it would be patently unfair to punish the women in preference to the men. They were merely following the example set them by the men.

Then there came the tragic conclusion that a people so devoid of spiritual understanding would be dashed to the ground. Utter ruin would come upon them. Their crass stupidity had led them into the morass of paganism: there seemed no hope for those who had committed such folly.

Though you, Israel, play the harlot, let not Judah become guilty. Go not to Gilgal. Neither go up to Beth-aven, nor swear, As Jehovah lives (Hos. 4:15).

Verse 15 is said by some commentators to have been an interpolation by an editor of Judah, but there is no sound reason for regarding it as other than the words of Hosea. Israel was sold to the spirit of whoredom, obsessed completely and irrevocably by the evil religion of Baal and its corrupting rites. The nation was unfaithful to God and was described as playing the harlot.

Judah had still the temple at Jerusalem, the divinely appointed priesthood and sacrificial system. It would have been a major tragedy if she had turned to the idolatry of the northern kingdom, and she was warned not to become guilty of the same offences. The golden calves, the fertility cult of Baal and Ashtoreth, the schismatic altars and the man-made priesthood had no significance for her and she should eschew any thought of them.

In further warning, the prophet bade her not to go up to Gilgal or Beth-aven, two of the major shrines of the north. Gilgal was the first site in the promised land at which the people encamped when they crossed the Jordan. It was there that Joshua renewed the rite of circumcision and the feast of the passover (Josh. 4 : 19; 5 : 9, 10). Bethel (i.e., "house of God"), which the prophet redesignated as Bethaven (i.e., "house of vanity"), was the place at which God had twice appeared to Jacob (Gen. 28 : 19; 35 : 1, 9) and at which the ark rested in the days of the judges (Jud. 20 : 26, 27). Here Jeroboam I placed one of his golden calves (1 Kings 12 : 29) and it consequently became one of the chief centres of the idolatrous worship. The Septuagint rather curiously substitutes On, the city of the sun in Egypt, for Bethaven, but there is no justification for this.

For some reason which is not apparent, Beersheba was not mentioned (see Amos 5 : 5), but there was probably an indirect reference to it. Beersheba means "the well of the oath", and Hosea warned Judah not to swear, "As Jehovah lives". It would indeed have been quite inappropriate to do so if the people of Judah had associated themselves with the idolatry of their brethren in the north.

BACKSLIDING ISRAEL

As a refractory heifer Israel has turned aside. Should Jehovah feed them like a lamb in a large place? Ephraim is joined to idols: let him alone. Their carouse is over: they have gone diligently a-whoring. Her rulers have loved shame thoroughly. A wind has wrapped them up in her wings, and they shall be ashamed because of their sacrifices (Hos. 4 : 16–19).

Israel's stupidity had been evidenced already, but her obstinacy or stubbornness was now indicated. Like a refractory heifer, she was to be tied up to prevent her roaming at will. Was it fitting, the prophet asked, that Jehovah should feed her like a lamb in a large meadow? The question was a rhetorical one, to which there could be only a negative reply. The freedom and prosperity indicated by the "large place" were not suitable for a nation which was so rebellious and ignorant of God.

There had been no indication of any repentance for the idolatry practised by the nation. Referring to her as Ephraim, God said that she was joined to idols and should be left alone. The word *atsabbim*, translated "idols", means both "images" and "sorrows", and there may be an implication that the idol-worship would eventually result in the sorrows caused by divine retribution. Those who accepted idols only merited the wrath of God, and the judgment of the Assyrian captivity was the only thing that would bring the nation to its senses.

Alluding to the bacchanalian character of the feasts of the Canaanite religion, Hosea declared that their carouse was over; they were a company of tipplers whose dissipation he virtually denounced. Excessive drinking was, in fact, one of the vices of his day and this was applicable generally, apart

E

from the orgies of the fertility rites. The carousal over, the prophet said that they pursued their lewd desires—they diligently went a-whoring. The very rulers were enamoured with infamy. The description was an apt one of the people's conduct in their religious exercises, but it was also true of the general behaviour in Israel. The body politic was corrupt.

In a remarkable figure, Hosea predicted the suddenness and violence with which the Assyrians would carry Israel into captivity. "A wind has wrapped them up in her wings" (or skirts), he said. The word *ruach* may refer to either "wind" or "spirit" but, in this instance, the former seems more appropriate. "The metaphor is that of a stormy wind, which has caught the people in its currents ("wings") and drives and buffets them helplessly in the direction in which it blows." Every opportunity for repentance had been given, but ultimately judgment proved unavoidable. Only then would the true character of their pagan religion dawn upon them. In exile they would have the time and opportunity to meditate upon their folly, and then would they be ashamed of their sacrifices to Baal and of the sinfulness of their practices.

CHAPTER 6

Approaching Judgment

THE arraignment of the nation, the statement of the case against the people and the indication of their fate having been given, the case against the priesthood and the royal house was presented. As the deeds of the court were reviewed, it is commonly thought that this oracle was uttered at Samaria, although there is no internal evidence to confirm this.

PRIEST AND KING

Hear this, O priests. Give heed, O house of Israel. Give ear, O house of the king. For the judgment is for you, because you have been a snare on Mizpah and a net spread out on Tabor. And they have made deep the pit of Shittim, but I will be the chastisement of them all (Hos. 5 : 1, 2).

If strictures were passed upon the nation, they were due also on those who should have been the instructors in morality and uprightness. It was because of their wilful failure and ineptitude that Israel had fallen so far into the morass of sin. Still using the imagery of the law-court, Hosea called upon priests, nation and royal house to pay attention and to hear the indictment. The usual word *kohen* was used for the priests, implying that they were, at least nominally, ministers of Jehovah (although not of the tribe of Levi and serving at shrines set up by Jeroboam): the word *kemarim*, referring to the priests of the Canaanite cult, was used later in ch. 10 : 5.

67

The house of Israel were presumably summoned as witnesses at the presentation of the case against the religious and political leaders, as well as to hear the case against themselves. Lehrman suggests that "the house of Israel" refers to the Sanhedrin, but this is not clear. Pusey (*op. cit.*, p. 55) considers that the king was "probably the unhappy Zechariah, a weak, pliant, self-indulgent, drunken scoffer, who after eleven years of anarchy, succeeded his father, only to be murdered" (2 Kings 15 : 10).

"The judgment is for you," warned the prophet. Instead of warning the people and guiding them into the right path, these evil leaders had led them into the depths of sin. Now the day of reckoning had come, and sentence was to be passed upon them. Three specific charges were laid by the plaintiff.

They had been a snare on Mizpah, i.e., the modern es-Salt or Ramoth Gilead. Mizpah was the site of Jacob's covenant with Laban (Gen. 31 : 45–53) and was a spot consecrated to God. It had since become one of the sacred places for the idolatrous worship of Baal and Ashtoreth. The accusation was that the leaders had been a snare on Mizpah. This was, of course, true in relation to their inducing the observance of the pagan rites there. In addition, however, there is a Jewish tradition that lyers in wait were set there to intercept and murder anyone journeying that way in order to worship at Jerusalem. It is certainly clear that every obstacle was put in the way of visits to Jerusalem for this purpose. The use of the word "snare" or "gin", i.e., a trap to catch the unwary, tends to confirm that the tradition had some substance.

They were also a net spread out on Tabor, ran the charge. Whereas the gin was a device made of two springs, the net was tethered to the ground with the object of entangling the quarry. Jerome mentions the snaring of birds on Tabor in his day. Mount Tabor still retains the same name today and is located in Galilee, west of the Jordan. It too became a centre of Baalism and, like Mizpah, was associated with the waylaying and murder of pilgrims to Jerusalem.

There is some doubt regarding the translation of verse 2,

but the rendering suggested above is in line with that adopted by a number of versions and is consistent with the charges in verse 1. The pit was a large hole carefully concealed by branches, etc., which gave way as soon as an animal stepped on them. It was, therefore, an apt symbol of the way in which the priests ensnared the people of God. Shittim was located in Moab and had also become a centre of Baal worship.

Despite all their evil machinations, Jehovah declared that He would be the chastisement of them all. Some versions render the sentence, "there is no correction for any of them," but this hardly seems to convey the sense of the words. These scheming priests had made their plans and laid their traps; the royal court had ignored the needs of the people and the responsibilities of the rulers towards them. They had all been guilty of misleading those over whom they had been appointed. There was no plea to present in reply to the charges, and sentence had, therefore, to be pronounced, and the punishment of them all was to be inflicted by Jehovah.

UNREPENTANT

I know Ephraim, and Israel is not hid from me. For now, O Ephraim, you have gone a-whoring, and Israel is defiled. Their doings will not suffer them to return to their God (Elohim): for the spirit of whoredoms is in their midst, and they know not Jehovah. But the pride of Israel shall testify to his face. Therefore shall Israel and Ephraim stumble in their iniquity. Judah shall also stumble with them (Hos. 5 : 3–5).

If chastisement was to come from Jehovah, it was not from someone unacquainted with Israel's guilt. He knew their inmost being, their open and their secret sins, and could read their very heart. No detail in Israel was hidden from Him. They had multiplied centres for the false worship and there they indulged in the polluting idolatry and sexual immorality. They had gone a-whoring, He declared, and Israel was defiled.

69

The licentious practices of the Canaanite shrines had rendered the people unclean.

It was impossible for them to return in penitence to God: their doings prevented them from taking this course. They were imprisoned by the grip of their past deeds and could not free themselves. They were so utterly habituated to evil practices that they could not break loose from them, even if they wished to do so. Honeycutt (*Hosea*, p. 28) says, "A man's deeds or actions become the obsessive, compulsive power of his life. They prevent him from making that quality of reflective appraisal which will lead to return and renewal. Sin robs man of his faculty for God and strength of will to obey God." Their lives were morally corrupt: "the spirit of whoredoms is in their midst," said the Divine Speaker. They were held in the grip of religious lust and immoral habits and had no desire for Jehovah. Indeed, they did not know Him. The pagan deities of nature had so filled their thoughts that all knowledge of the true God had been dissipated.

In the assize which had been metaphorically set up, therefore, Jehovah, "the pride of Israel", would not be their advocate, but would Himself testify to their face. It was legal terminology: God Himself would give evidence in His own court, which would condemn the guilty nation. They were without defence and would stumble when the sentence was pronounced.

Judah had been warned against adopting the practices of the northern kingdom, but she was still guilty before God, and the prophet declared that Judah would also stumble with Israel when sentence was pronounced.

TOO LATE

They shall go with their flocks and herds to seek Jehovah; but they shall not find Him: he has withdrawn Himself from them. They have dealt treacherously against Jehovah, for they have begotten strange children. Now shall the new moon devour them with their portions (Hos. 5 : 6, 7).

The basic religion of the northern kingdom—as distinct from the Canaanite religion subsequently adopted—was fundamentally the worship of Jehovah. The golden calves and other features, which Jeroboam I had introduced for expediency, were certainly extraneous, but the people imagined that they were worshipping Jehovah, albeit at a different centre from that Divinely appointed at Jerusalem. Their offerings and sacrifices were brought to be offered to Jehovah. Gradually, however, the people were corrupted by Baalism and the sensual nature worship superseded the service of Jehovah.

Hosea pictured the people wending their way to the sacred shrines with their flocks and herds, with the obvious intention of sacrificing to Jehovah. Yet the smoke of their sacrifices invoked no response from heaven. They sought for God but could not find Him, because He had withdrawn from them. He was no longer accessible to them and was deaf to their petitions.

He stated the reason for His withdrawal as their unfaithfulness and their begetting of strange children. In adopting the worship of Baal, Israel had committed spiritual adultery. The nation had been espoused to Jehovah, but she had proved unfaithful and had turned to paganism and its debasing ritual. She had been unfaithful to Him.

The result of her relationship with the false gods was that children had been born through the adulterous union. The words were metaphorical, but it was a fact that a generation had grown up in the superstitious and licentious ritual, who knew little of Jehovah. They were not His "children", but the fruit of a spiritual adultery, and more estranged from Jehovah even than their parents.

The new moon was always recognised in the religious calendar. Apart from the observances attached to it, the new moon fixed the dates of certain of the festivals. But the new moon was to devour them. They would, in future, wait for the new moon, not with eager anticipation, but with increasing fear and in the consciousness that the advent of the plundering horde of invaders could not long be postponed. The next

71

month might see their coming. Judgment could not be delayed. Their portions, i.e., the land allocated to them, would be taken by the enemy at the same time. Material possessions were doomed. Their fate was sealed.

THE SIGNAL

Blow the cornet in Gibeah, the trumpet in Ramah. Cry aloud at Bethaven. Behind you, O Benjamin (Hos. 5 : 8).

The invasion, of which a hint had been given, grew steadily nearer. Rezin of Syria and Pekah of Israel joined forces to attack Judah. Ahaz, besieged in Jerusalem, appealed to the Assyrians for help and sent gifts to Tiglath-pileser. The latter acceded to the request and routed the army of Syria, slew Rezin and captured Damascus (2 Kings 16 : 5–9).

The prophet saw the gathering storm and called to the watchmen on the hills of Gibeah and Ramah to sound the warning blast on cornet and trumpet to set the people on the alert. He bade the guard at Bethaven or Bethel to voice the shout of alarm. Both southern and northern kingdoms would be warned by the blast from the towns set on their eminences and would be prepared for the foe.

In thought, he heard the tribal battle-cry of Benjamin, "Behind you, O Benjamin", rallying the forces to prepare for the conflict. Bethel was a border-town between Benjamin and Ephraim and stood on the road along which the invasion was liable to occur. The judgment upon the nation had commenced.

EPHRAIM'S FATE

Ephraim shall be a desolation in the day of correction. Among the tribes of Israel I make known what shall surely be. The princes of Judah have become like those who remove the landmark. I will pour out my wrath upon them like water. Ephraim is oppressed and broken in judgment, because he wilfully went after vanity (Hos. 5 : 9–11).

Judicial punishment (or correction) was to be meted out upon Israel. Already the invader had penetrated to the southern border of the country and when the forces swept through, the land would be completely devastated. The gathering of the tribes of Israel would be fruitless. God made it clear that what He had decreed would surely come to pass. The prophecy apparently looked on to the campaign of Shalmaneser and the capture of Samaria and the deportation of Israel (2 Kings 17 : 3–6). The warning had been given, but there had been no expression of penitence, and the blow ultimately fell.

The historian records that, when Jehovah punished Israel and removed them out of His sight, He left the nation of Judah, but that they also, ignoring the lesson, followed the same course as Israel (2 Kings 17 : 18, 19). When the people of Israel had been deported by the Assyrians, Judah seized the opportunity of expropriating territory which had belonged to members of the northern kingdom. The prophet pertinently likened them to those who removed the landmark.

Boundary stones marked the borders of properties and the law forbade the removal of these landmarks (Deut. 19 : 14), but unscrupulous men avariciously encroached upon the paternal inheritances of others. They ought to have taken warning at the fate of Israel, but they were only concerned about making the greatest conceivable gains out of their neighbours' plight. At the same time, they emulated Israel in the latter's sin.

There could be only one answer, and Jehovah declared that He would pour out His wrath upon them like a swollen stream. He would no more tolerate evil in Judah than in Israel and He showed His anger at their despicable conduct.

They might well have realised the significance of Israel's fall. Ephraim was oppressed and broken (or dashed in pieces) by judgment. The hand of God had fallen heavily upon the country and the nation had been utterly crushed. The nation had provoked the punishment; they wilfully went after vanity, i.e., after the idols of the heathen (cf. Jer. 18 : 15). The A.V.

"willingly walked after the commandment" is generally applied to the worship of the golden calves at the command of Jeroboam and his successors, but the Peshitta and the Septuagint rendering of "wilfully went after vanity" may convey the true sense of the prophecy.

As for me, I am like a moth to Ephraim, and like rottenness to the house of Judah. When Ephraim saw his sickness and Judah his wound, then went Ephraim to the Assyrian and sent to the warlike king. But he is unable to heal you or to relieve you of your wound. For I will be like a lion to Ephraim, and like a young lion to the house of Judah. I, even I, will rend and go away. I will carry off and none shall rescue. I will return again to my place, until they acknowledge their guilt and seek my face. In their affliction they will seek me earnestly (Hos. 5 : 12–15).

The lax morality and sexual impurity resulting from a retrograde religion naturally had a debilitating effect upon the whole nation of Israel: the body politic was rotten. But Jehovah now revealed that another influence was secretly at work, which had a far more destructive effect and which led to the internal dissolution and punitive crushing. Using extraordinary metaphors, He described Himself as the hidden destructive power in the nation—and not only in Israel, but in Judah also.

"I am like a moth to Ephraim," he declared, "and like rottenness to the house of Judah." The moth in a garment slowly and almost imperceptibly eats the cloth away. It proceeds stealthily and unhinderedly, but completely effectually. The dry rot, or caries, in wood proceeds at an even slower pace, but nothing can arrest its progress. Wool and wood are eventually destroyed. So, God declared, would He destroy the power and vitality of Israel and Judah. The former proved incapable of delivering themselves from the Assyrians. If the decay continued longer in the case of Judah, that nation was

74

also ultimately unable to resist the power of the Babylonians. The people of both kingdoms were removed from their lands into captivity. Punishment was complete.

Taking Hosea's bold imagery of moth and caries, Pusey (*op. cit.*, p. 61) writes, "So God visits the soul with different distresses, bodily or spiritual. He impairs, little by little, health of body, or fineness of understanding; or allows luke-warmness and distaste for the things of God to creep over the soul. These are the gnawing of the moth." It is a serious thing to come under the judicial hand of God.

Both Israel and Judah were aware of their weakness and of the need for help, and it might well have been expected that, in their extremity, they would have turned to Jehovah for healing of the internal cancer which was destroying them and for protection from the external foe who threatened them. Throughout the history of the nation, it was Jehovah who had been their deliverer and help. Yet they seem to have given no thought to the only One who could save them. Instead, they engaged in political negotiations with their most dangerous enemy, for both kingdoms turned in desperation to Assyria.

Ahaz of Judah sought the help of Tiglath-pileser when threatened by Syria and Israel (2 Kings 16 : 7). Menahem of Israel followed a similar course in bribing the Assyrians to withdraw from his land (2 Kings 15 : 19, 20). Hosea of Israel later similarly came to an arrangement with Shalmaneser (2 Kings 17 : 3). Neither nation seemed to realise the folly and futility of their actions. If it was Jehovah who inflicted th wounds, it was quite impossible for the heathen power to he them. Furthermore, the course they so injudiciously follow only provided Assyria with a pretext for interference in th countries.

The Scriptures state that Ephraim sent to "king Jareb," "the warlike king". No king of this name was known an has been suggested that it was a metaphor for Sennach Tiglath-pileser, Sargon or Shalmaneser. It is more prob however, that the word was used in a general sense in ence to the warlike character of Assyria's rulers. In any

75

the prophet indicated the utter inability of this king to help the suppliants: he was unable to heal or to relieve the kingdoms of their wound. Since God had inflicted the wound, no human skill could effect a cure.

Jehovah made it clear that He was the destroyer. "I will be like a lion to Ephraim," He said, "and like a young lion to the house of Judah." Cheyne (*op. cit.*, p. 76) points out that "Hebrew has at least five words for 'lion'; of the two selected here, the first describes this terror of ancient Palestine as a roarer (so 13 : 7), the second as covered with a mane." The Septuagint substitutes "panther" for the first, but "lion" appears to be a more correct rendering. There was no escape from the Divine destroyer. He announced that He would rend and carry off the prey. The instruments He used might be the Assyrians, but the direction came from a Divine source. None could rescue those whom He had destined to destruction. When the lion seized its prey, no one could snatch it from the mouth of the ravager. The rending or tearing and the suffering inflicted were His purpose for a guilty people.

As the lion returned to its lair after seizing its prey, so Jehovah declared that He would return to His place (i.e., His temple—see Mic. 1 : 3). He had inflicted condign punishment upon his people (and Hosea regarded it as a *fait accompli*, although it had not then actually occurred), and He now withdrew until the consciousness of their guilt and need was borne home to them. He waited until they acknowledged their sin and sought His face in contrition and repentance. Their experience of suffering and their exile in a strange land would surely drive them to seek the cause of their affliction. When they became conscious of their sinfulness, they would be forced to return penitently to the One against whom they had sinned. Their punishment was simply a means of awakening them and bringing them back to God. When they discerned the cause of their wounds, they would, He declared, seek Him earnestly.

One of the means employed by God to bring His people back to Himself has always been the sufferings of life. In days

76

of prosperity a spirit of independence often develops, but in days of adversity the believer is forced back with a sense of need into the arms of the Eternal Lover. In divine wisdom, He chastens in order to restore to His love once more. This was His purpose for Israel.

CHAPTER 7

Shallow Repentance

THE sufferings of Israel and their ultimate expulsion from their own land, so clearly predicted by Hosea, might reasonably be interpreted by a superficial observer as an indication of God's rejection of a reprobate race. They had dishonoured Him, corrupted His worship, indulged in idolatrous infidelity to Him, disregarded His claims and ignored His power. They had justifiably been condemned and it might have been anticipated that they had now been finally excluded from Divine blessing. This, however, would be a serious misinterpretation of the purposes of God. The castigation inflicted was in punishment for sin; the expulsion from the land was to deprive them of the shrines and the idolatrous system of worship; the exile in Assyria was to afford them the opportunity of meditating upon their guilt and of turning in repentance to God.

Whatever purpose there may be, the object of trial and tribulation for the believer is always to bring him back to communion with God. So Israel might have been expected to turn humbly to Jehovah with a plea for pardon and forgiveness.

THE RETURN

Come, let us return to Jehovah: for he has torn and he will heal us. He has smitten and he will bind us up. After two

*days he will revive us and on the third day he will raise us up
and we shall live before him. Let us know, let us press on to
know Jehovah, His going forth is as sure as the dawn. He will
come to us as the heavy rain, as the latter rain which waters
the earth (Hos. 6 : 1–3).*

The door had been left open for a repentant people to return in heart to Jehovah. If, in humble sincerity, they had
come before Him to confess their guilt and to seek by Divine
help to amend their ways, His compassion would surely have
descended to their need and His love would have restored
their communion with Himself. They certainly decided to
return, but amazingly without the slightest admission of guilt
and apparently without the slightest awareness that any wrong
had been committed. It seems almost incredible that the
lesson so laboriously taught should have been so utterly ineffective. No impression whatsoever had been made upon
their heart or conscience.

"Come, let us return to Jehovah," they exhorted one another in sheer presumption, as though no shadow of a cloud
lay between themselves and Him. There was no consciousness
of sin and no expression of regret for the sorrow caused to the
Almighty. Cut off from Baal and Ashtoreth, it seemed natural
to them to seek Jehovah.

Of one fact they had become aware. If they had been torn
or wounded, it was Jehovah who had caused it. There seems
to have been no enquiry as to the reason for the infliction:
they merely sought a cure. God had inflicted the wound and,
confidently they assured themselves, He would heal. They had
at least realised that He was the only physician to whom they
could turn, but they wanted no more than healing. There was
no pledge of a change of life or conduct, no declared intent
that, in future, Him alone would they serve. There was no
rejection of the pagan religion or regret for the immoral practices of the past. There was no sorrow of heart. Their words
were the empty phraseology of unreality and insincerity. Before condemning their arrant folly, we ought to ensure that we

79

are not guilty of comparable insincerity in our approach to God and that every known sin is judged and put away before we seek fellowship with Him.

Jehovah had torn and, with the utmost assurance, they claimed that He would heal them. He had smitten them, but He would bind up the wound. They had no doubt as to His willingness. They could take their time in considering the matter, but they imagined that God was graciously awaiting their request and would respond immediately.

After two days He would revive them, they declared, and on the third day He would raise them up and they would live before Him. They virtually demanded—as though entitled to it—a speedy release from their trials. God was able and He would do it. The expression "two days" and "third day" were the substance of the Hebrew idiom meaning "after a short while". There may have been a deeper significance in the expression, however, Baal died and rose again on the third day. Of Adonis the same was claimed. A number of commentators see a prediction of the resurrection of Christ in the words, but they do not seem capable of sustaining this meaning. The people of Israel regarded themselves as a sick man, who had been wounded. They looked to Jehovah for healing. After two days they anticipated that they would be healed and on the third day that they would emerge from their troubles. The concept was a foolish one for no wounded man is healed so rapidly. Those who read into the words an indication of a national revival of Israel go beyond the obvious significance. The rabbinical interpretation was that the numbers referred to the three captivities—Egyptian, Babylonian and Roman—but this fanciful interpretation has little to commend it.

When Jehovah had dealt with their needs, they asserted that they would live before Him, i.e., under His protection, as if it was possible to live in fellowship with a holy God while sin was still on the conscience. This, of course, is the error made by many Christians today. The smallest sin is a barrier to communion with Christ, and fellowship can be restored only when the defilement has been removed.

Despite the presumptuous attitude they had demonstrated, there did seem a recognition of the fact that their calamities were due to living without the knowledge of Jehovah, i.e., without an acknowledgment experientially of His supreme lordship and sufficiency. The knowledge of God implied an appreciation of His character and dignity, an understanding of the proper relationship to Him, and a willingness to surrender all to Him. Whether all this was involved in Israel's cry, "Let us know, let us press on to know Jehovah is doubtful." It may be rather, as Mays (*op. cit.*, p. 95) considers, that the words expressed "the desperation of the nation's need, their terrified frantic plan to undertake the 'knowledge of God' as an emergency measure." They anticipated, in consequence, that Jehovah would fulfill for them the same functions as Baal had allegedly done, supplying rain and ensuring the fertility of the land.

Their resolution was hasty and ill-considered and unaccompanied by the necessary ingredient of confession. They confidently declared that Jehovah's going forth was as certain as the dawn. While this was assuredly true and, as certainly as morning succeeds the night, God does come to the aid of the repentant, these presumptuous sinners could not claim that it would be verified for them.

They claimed that He would come to them as the heavy rain of winter and the latter rain of spring. These two rains, the first at the beginning of the season and the latter at the end, were essential to a good harvest. These were the gifts which they had attributed to Baal, but were now equally prepared in their volatility to attribute to Jehovah. As a description of His character, the symbolism was perfectly apt, but how could they expect it to be applicable for them? As one writer remarks, "Their confidence is excessive; they presume on God's forgiveness without complying with His conditions."

SUPERFICIALITY

What shall I do to you, O Ephraim? What shall I do to you, O Judah? For your piety is like a morning cloud and like the dew which goes early away (Hos. 6 : 4).

Jehovah's reply revealed that their shallow unreality was not veiled from Him, and He associated Judah with Ephraim in His exposure of their emptiness. Their confidence in His immediate response in face of unconfessed sin was sadly misplaced. Their expressed desire to know Him was no more than an unreal sciolism. Their implication of a national revival was completely meaningless. They were utterly unworthy of Him.

Yet His heart yearned after them still. They were His people and He longed for the sincere devotion of loyal subjects. In a lamentation over the transitory character of their change of attitude, He cried, "What shall I do to you?" He had been their constant Benefactor, their Saviour, their Protector. He had proved Himself their sufficiency in all the varied circumstances of life. What other method could He employ to win back their loyalty? Their empty and hastily conceived resolutions meant nothing to One who sought the reciprocation of His love to them. What more could He do than He had already done? He had chosen them from the nations of the earth in arbitrary sovereignty; He had given them a land for which they had not laboured; He had blessed them with material prosperity, but they had discounted every gift and had attributed His goodness to Baal. Even now, when they had turned to Him for help, there was no sincerity in their protestations of faithfulness. What could He do to awaken the soul's deep desire?

They had likened Him to the constant dawn and the early and latter rain on which the harvest depended. Taking His imagery also from the climatic conditions of the country, Jehovah described their transient piety (or loving kindness) as like the morning mist, which was seen for a brief while and then disappeared (cf. Jas 4 : 14). The "morning cloud" was a dense mass of vapour borne in at night by the summer winds from the Mediterranean, which vanished with the heat of the morning sun (Isa. 18 : 4). The welcome dew, distilled in the night, clung in iridescent beauty to every blade of grass, but its promise evaporated even more rapidly than the mist.

So was their expression of piety, said Jehovah. It was as evanescent and lacking in substance as the morning mist and evaporated as quickly as the early dew. This was not true devotion, but empty words. Above everything else, God seeks reality and sincerity.

GOD'S DEALINGS

Therefore have I hewn them by prophets; I have slain them by the words of my mouth and your judgments go forth like the light. For I desire piety and not sacrifice; and the knowledge of God (Elohim) more than burnt offerings. But they, like Adam, transgressed the covenant; there they dealt treacherously against me (Hos. 6 : 5–7).

The attitude displayed by the nation was nothing new: their capriciousness had previously invoked Divine interposition. As a sculptor hews the rock into shape to use for his purpose, so Jehovah had hewn them by prophets, endeavouring to fashion them to His will, but the efforts had been unavailing. He had metaphorically or literally slain them with the words of His mouth, for a destructive power was ascribed to the Word of God (Isa. 11 : 4; Jer. 5 : 14): by implication, physical tribulations had followed the preaching of the prophets in the form of war, exile, famine and pestilence.

There could be no dubiety about the meaning of the Divine actions. The verdict was as clear as the day. The judgments pronounced upon them by Jehovah issued forth with the piercing effect of the lightning's flash. How ill-conceived was their exuberant confidence: rather should they have trembled in fear and awe of the Almighty.

Not only shallowness but vacillation seemed endemic to Israel, and it was essential to make the requirements for God perfectly clear. The prophet implied that, conscious of Jehovah's disapproval, the people might well seek to propitiate Him by sacrifice and offering. This was not the answer. God sought true devotion—dutiful love or sincere piety— first:

83

this was of far greater importance than sacrifices. The Lord Jesus Christ emphasised the same point, quoting the same words, in His earthly ministry (Matt. 9 : 13; 12 : 7). The sacrificial act without the true morality of life was inconsistent and valueless. This was the lesson which Saul failed to learn centuries ago (1 Sam. 15 : 22). The sacrifice implied furthermore the subsequent sharing of the sacrificial meal, in which typically God Himself participated, thereby establishing communion between the worshipper and the Eternal. There could be no communion with God without a consistency of life.

The knowledge of God was of greater moment than the burnt or ascending offerings Israel were ready to bring. The holocaust was entirely for God, but in the presentation of the whole animal to Jehovah, the worshipper identified himself and his absolute devotion to God : it was an act of supreme adoration and worship. How could God accept that in the light of the shallow insincerity of their protestations? The first requirement was the knowledge of Him—an apprehension of His character and ways and a consequent heartfelt dedication of self to Him.

It is interesting to note that a somewhat similar saying was ascribed to Buddha (although the vital substance was naturally missing). He said, "If man live a hundred years, and engage the whole of his time and attention in religious offerings to the gods, sacrificing elephants and horses and other life, all this is not equal to one act of pure love in saving life." Jehovah's words, of course, went much farther and tacitly required a complete dedication to Him.

The prophecy emphasised the contrast between Jehovah's requirements and Israel's tergiversation. They were just like other men, who were addicted to sin and vice and had been responsible for breach of the covenant with Jehovah. The Hebrew stated that they, like Adam, had transgressed the covenant. If this rendering is accepted, the reference must clearly be assumed to be the first man's disobedience in Eden and his violation of the only commandment given to him. Some versions render the words "at Adam", thereby linking

84

the statement with the miracle at Adam, where the waters of the Jordan were cut off while the Israelites crossed the river nearer Jericho (Josh. 3 : 16), but the relevance of this is not clear. The more probable meaning was that Israel, from whom so much more might have been expected, had proved no different from other men and had failed in similar fashion.

"Implying a gesture of indignation," as one writer says, "the divine speaker points to the northern kingdom as the scene of unfaithfulness," for "there", He said, "they dealt treacherously against me." The allusion could scarcely have been to the town of Adam. It was in the land of Israel that the infidelity had been demonstrated: it was there, where Baalism had held sway, that the people had been unfaithful to Jehovah.

EVIL SPOTS

Gilead is a city of workers of iniquity, tracked with bloody footprints. As bands of robbers lie in wait for a man, so do the company of priests; they murder on the road to Shechem; they commit outrages (Hos. 6 : 8, 9).

God selected two towns in Israel as outstanding illustrations of the infamous conduct of the country. The town of Gilead (as distinct from the region) was only referred to here and in Jud. 10 : 17. Cheyne (*op. cit.*, p. 80) says that the Gileadites, half-civilised mountaineers, seem to have been distinguished for their ferocity (cf., 2 Kings 15 : 25)." Certainly this is confirmed by Hosea, which described the city as one of evildoers and tracked with bloody footprints (cf. 1 Kings 2 : 5). It was evidently the haunt of lawless assassins and stained with the crimes they had committed.

It was no safer for the traveller along the road to Shechem. This was one of the cities of refuge (Josh. 21 : 21), but it became notorious for the highway robberies committed by its citizens, in consequence of which Abimelech rased it to the ground (Jud. 9 : 25, 45). It had been rebuilt and stood on the road from Samaria to Bethel, the principal sanctuary of Israel, so that many passed that way. Here a company of evil priests, like a gang of bandits, lay in wait for the unwary traveller, and this depraved troop murdered, raped and outraged at will. The word *zimmah,* translated "outrages", referred particularly to crimes of immorality.

This was the character of the nation which professed allegiance to Jehovah and now sought His help in their time of trouble.

DEFILEMENT

In the house of Israel I have seen a horrible thing: there is the harlotry of Ephraim. Israel is defiled. For you also, O Judah, a harvest is appointed, when I turned the captivity of my people (Hos. 6 : 10, 11).

If Gilead and Shechem exemplified the depravity and wickedness of the land, Jehovah declared that He had seen a horrifying thing in Israel—literally, something to make the hair stand on end. In the holy land, which He had bestowed upon His chosen people, there was harlotry. What was envisaged was not merely the spiritual adultery typified by idolatry, but the actual abominations practised in the name of religion. The immorality and prostitution of the fertility cult were a pollution of the land and anathema to God. It was horrifying that such things should be found in Israel and He indignantly declared that Israel was defiled. It seems almost incredible that the conditions described should have been possible.

Judah had not escaped the infection of her neighbour. Consequently a harvest had been appointed for the southern kingdom. What she had sown, she would reap. Nothing escaped the Divine eye and it was His purpose to mete out retribution to guilty Judah also.

The last clause of verse 11 belongs more properly to ch. 7 : 1 and is a colloquialism for the reversal of misfortunes. Jehovah would eventually release His people from their captivity.

CHAPTER 8

Moral Degradation

THE conditions which Hosea went on to describe—the open breakdown of law and order, of morality and civil authority—lead to the conclusion that Jeroboam II's death had occurred and that the period covered was that following his death up to the capture of Samaria by the Assyrians. The national degeneracy and the approaching state of anarchy were clearly indicated, yet there was still no consciousness of sin on the part of the people. They approached Jehovah as they would have done Baal, without the slightest awareness that the character of their lives and conduct was in any way pertinent. Their degradation was complete.

UNWORTHY PEOPLE

When I would heal Israel, the iniquity of Ephraim is revealed and the wickedness of Samaria; for they commit falsehood; the thief breaks in, and the troop of robbers spoils outside (Hos. 7 : 1).

It is usually considered that the last clause of Hos. 6 : 11 should be attached to Hos. 7 : 1. Ewald renders the verse perhaps rather more clearly, "When I turn the fortunes of my people, when I heal Israel, then will be manifest Ephraim's guilt and Samaria's wickedness, how they practise falsehood, and the thief comes in, and bandits roam abroad without."

The prophet anticipated the day of Israel's deliverance,

when her captivity came to an end, and there may be a glimpse of a fulfilment still future. When Jehovah determined to "turn their captivity" and to bring healing to them, however, the enormity of their wickedness became more apparent than before. The iniquity of Ephraim and the wickedness of Samaria were now revealed. What was previously done in secret was now shamelessly committed in public. Conscience had been blunted and there was no attempt to conceal the disgraceful misconduct.

Their whole behaviour was summed up in the statement that they practised falsehood. Their sophistry was evident in their approach to God while still actively engaged in evil practices. They spoke of knowing Him while they impenitently pursued their habitual course. They needed the healing Jehovah purposed, but their malady was moral and not physical.

With no authority to prevent him, the thief broke into the dwellings to take what he chose. While the words were doubtless intended to be taken literally, there may have been a typical significance in them as well. These people had no protection against evil; having dispensed with moral standards themselves, they were easily influenced by any attack upon the mind or heart. Any thief could rob them of faith and honesty and integrity, as well as of material possessions. A sudden appeal from without and they would fall.

The prophecy depicted not only the thief breaking in, but a gang of bandits roaming the streets outside. Highway robbery was common; law was not held in respect; who, therefore would be concerned with right or wrong? The country was corrupt and civil administration had completely failed. Fraud, theft and violence were rampant and mendacity was a characteristic of the nation.

EVIL DISCERNED

But they do not consider in their hearts that I remember all their wickedness. Now have their deeds encompassed them; they are before my face (Hos. 7 : 2).

88

The erosion of honesty and uprightness had resulted in a shameful indifference to the heinousness of sin. Immersed in their evil deeds, the people no longer paused to consider their ultimate accountability, nor the fact that their actions were being recorded by the One who observed all. Since sin had ceased to shock them, they foolishly concluded that nothing mattered and that they would never be held responsible for what they did. They did not imagine that Jehovah took account of their wicked deeds, nor that their affected piety was an insult to Him. But they were now entangled in their sins and unable to release themselves from them. Their iniquity encompassed them like the insurmountable walls of a prison. And if they presumptuously ignored their guilt and affected to call upon God, He remembered and their doings were always before Him. Their callous indifference to Divine standards and to their own accountability was utter folly.

A CORRUPT COURT

They make the king glad with their wickedness, and the princes with their lies. They are all adulterers, like an oven heated by the baker, who ceases from heating after he has kneaded the dough until it is leavened. In the day of our king, the princes became sick with the fever of wine; he stretched out his hand with scorners (Hos. 7 : 3–5).

Justice and righteousness should derive from the highest authority and the example of the people should be set by the royal court. Yet the prophecy disclosed that corruption existed in the highest circles of the land. The king and his court were abandoned to sensual pleasures and unrestrained debauchery. Jeroboam II had evidently died and the country was now ruled by his son, Zechariah, a profligate and unworthy character, whose murder was already being planned.

Instead of insisting on the maintenance of standards by the court, the king delighted in the misdeeds of the evil characters with whom he surrounded himself. The more degraded their bacchanalian orgies, the greater his pleasure. The princes, who encouraged the monstrous excesses, rejoiced in the duplicity and pernicious practices of their followers. The mephitic atmosphere of the court was appalling.

They were habitual adulterers, said the prophet, constantly inflamed by lust. In their uncontrolled passions they were like a baker's oven, raised to a certain heat until the kneaded dough was leavened. The oven was a structure of burnt clay in which the fire was built, the flat cakes of dough being spread on the walls. The fire was left to smoulder until the fermentation of the dough was complete, and then it was re-kindled to a greater heat once more. So the burning passions of these debauchees, after satisfaction, remained dormant only until fresh opportunities afforded themselves, and then the fires of lust broke out once more.

Some expositors see the baker as a figure of the evil imagination of these adulterers but, while this is appropriate, it is not really necessary to press the symbolism so far. Others have interpreted the whole imagery of the oven, the dough and the baker, in the context of the conspiracy to assassinate the king, the evil desires being those, not of the court but of the murderous conspirators. Verses 3 and 4 seem to hold together, however, and to relate primarily to the debauchery of the royal court.

There seems little doubt that Cheyne is right in concluding that, in verse 6, the figurative description is interrupted by an actual incident from real life. It was a special day for the king, possibly his coronation day, but more probably his birthday. The conspirators had made their plans to assassinate him, and they adopted the stratagem of making king and courtiers drunk. The princes or court officials were so intoxicated as to be "sick with the fever of wine", leaving the sovereign entirely defenceless.

There was nothing to prevent the revolutionaries executing their *coup d'état*. The drunken king stretched out his hand to his boon companions, not realising that he was with mockers. It was apparently his last carousal and the sounds of revelry would never again resound in his palace. Zechariah was the fourth generation of the house of Jehu and with his murder by Shallum, the dynasty came to an end (2 Kings 15 : 8–12). Hosea's prediction was fulfilled.

THE PLOT SUCCEEDS

For their inward part is like an oven, their heart burns in them while they lie in wait. Their anger smokes all night; in the morning it blazes like a flaming fire. They are all hot as an oven and they devour their judges. All their kings have fallen. None of them calls to me (Hos. 7 : 6, 7).

Still describing the conspiracy against the king, the prophecy declared that the conspirators were inwardly like an oven. The hot passion consumed them like an oven fire while they lay in wait. Their preparations had been made, but their hatred was almost uncontrollable and smoked all night. They slept fitfully, nursing their murderous schemes until the morning.

When the new day dawned, their anger burst out against their destined victim. In their impatience they could hardly wait to bring their intrigues to a successful conclusion. They were as hot as an oven, which had been prepared for baking.

They devoured or destroyed their rulers, declared the prophet. All their kings had fallen. Shallum's murder of Zechariah was followed by Menahem's murder of Shallum (2 Kings 15 : 14). Four regicides occurred in four decades. Indeed, of Israel's 17 kings, only 8 died a natural death, the other 9 being dethroned and murdered by their successors. It was no wonder that the kingdom sank into chaos and anarchy.

Yet, in such conditions, no one called upon Jehovah. It was a sad commentary on the irreligious state of the nation. There may have been a superficial recognition of God; sacrifices may have been offered to Him; but there was no true "knowledge of God". They were completely out of touch with Him.

EPHRAIM'S FOLLY

Ephraim, he has mixed himself with the peoples; Ephraim

*is a cake not turnèd. Strangers have devoured his strength,
and he knows it not; gray hairs are sprinkled upon him, yet
he knows it not. The pride of Israel testifies to his face; yet
they do not return to Jehovah their God (Elohim), nor seek
him for all this (Hos. 7 : 8–10).*

The exposure of the blatant corruption of the royal court
and the prediction of the end of the monarchy were followed
by a denunciation of the international policy of Israel and of
the inevitable political decay of the nation. With a corrupt
administration, there could obviously be no political stability,
yet negotiations aimed at ensuring the kingdom's security had
long been continuing. Alliances with powerful neighbours,
however, could only provide pretexts to these greater states
for interference in the affairs of the smaller country. In addition,
such treaties had the detrimental effect of introducing foreign
customs and modes of living into the country. Israel was
situated on the roads connecting great empires and traders and
merchants naturally brought new concepts to the little state.

Hosea's condemnation of the procedures adopted was expressed in unusual terms, first by imagery from the culinary
realm. Ephraim had mixed himself with the peoples, he
declared. The primary connotation of the term was found in
the religious sphere: it applied, for example, to the mixing of
the oil and flour in the meal offerings. It was also, rather
intriguingly, used in relation to the origin of Babel. The
accusation was that the nation had so mingled with their
heathen neighbours as to affect their national pristine purity
and their sanctification to Jehovah.

It had always been the Divine purpose that Israel should be
separated from the nations of the world. She was to dwell
alone (Num. 23 : 9; Deut. 33 : 28). She belonged to Jehovah
and He was her sufficiency. There was no need to seek the
help of pagan powers in her supposed extremity. He was
capable of protecting His own people and His own possessions. Their mixing with the other nations was an expression
of lack of confidence in Him. The courting of Egypt or of

92

Assyria was virtually an act of disloyalty to the One who had separated them to Himself.

Unfortunately this is so often the attitude of the believer. He cannot believe that God is capable of meeting his need and solving his problems. He feels compelled to use his own initiative to find a way out of the difficulty, or to address his own intellect to find a solution to the problem. The anxieties and worries with which he burdens himself are so totally unnecessary if God is sufficient. It is sheer lack of faith and trust in a loving Father.

In equally startling imagery, the prophet declared that Ephraim was half-baked, a cake not turned. The picture is of the flat cake which was cooked first on one side and then turned to be cooked on the other. It was the apt symbol of the nation's inconsistencies. One expositor sees in the figure the unequal distribution of wealth, so that there were extremes of poverty and riches, but the reference seems principally to the character of the people and the folly of their frantic intrigues with various powers and particularly with Egypt and Assyria—now hot, now cold, in fact half-baked.

Strangers had devoured Ephraim's strength, said Hosea, without his being aware of it. The commercial and political intercourse with other nations had destroyed the character of Israel. Furthermore, the ravaging of the country by stronger powers and the heavy tribute exacted by Hazael, Benhadad, Tiglath-pileser and others had weakened the kingdom far more than had probably been realised.

Pathetically the prophet added that gray hairs were sprinkled upon Ephraim and he did not know it. The national decrepitude had crept upon them almost unobserved. The sapping of the national vitality was well portrayed as the advance of senility without the awareness of the nation. The body politic bore all the marks of a dying nation. It was moving relentlessly and helplessly towards the end, like a man who had dissipated his strength and had become prematurely old. The nation's plight was tragic.

Are the words not applicable to many Christians of our

twentieth century? Spiritual vitality has diminished, power has disappeared, perhaps through compromise with the world and alliance with those from whom we should be separate. Inconsistency, occupation with the secular rather than the spiritual, and the use of talents and faculties for the acquisition of the material and temporal, rather than for the abiding realities which never fail, may all be responsible for the diminution of power and spiritual life. Hosea's words may still be relevant today.

The pride of Israel, i.e. Jehovah Himself, bore witness against His people. In the light of their inconsistency and their intrigues, their immorality and apostasy, He gave them warning. Yet, in their complacency, they completely ignored God and His Word. They were confident of finding their own solution to their problems and were, therefore, quite unmindful of Him. The chastisement which had been threatened did not disturb their equilibrium; the difficulties which they were currently experiencing had no effect upon them. They did not return to God nor seek Him, despite their obvious need. It seemed as though they were almost oblivious to His presence.

JEHOVAH ACTS

Ephraim is like a silly dove, without understanding, calling to Egypt, going to Assyria. As soon as they go, I will spread over them my net. I will bring them down like the fowls of heaven. I will chastise them, as their congregation has heard (Hos. 7 : 11, 12).

Still pursuing the subject of Israel's international policy and foreign diplomacy, Hosea described the kingdom as a silly dove without understanding, calling to Egypt, going to Assyria. Like a harmless dove, trying to escape the attack of a bird of prey, flying hither and thither in panic, and without any idea of the best thing to do, Ephraim had swung to and fro like a pendulum. At one moment they sought help from Egypt, at another they sought to appease Assyria. There was no sound judgment, no evidence of any careful assessment of the position. It was an inane, addlepated policy. Any attempt by a small nation to play off greater powers one against another must always be a dangerous game to play and, in any case, it was one that only of the highest experience could play. It was folly for a politically inexperienced nation to indulge in it.

While they were so engaged, Israel did not observe that Jehovah was also taking a part. Metaphorically, He stood with a fowler's net in His hand, waiting to snare the silly dove of Ephraim as it flew to and fro. When the opportunity arose, He would cast the net over them and bring them down like the birds of the air. (The net is probably a symbol of the captivity.) They could not escape His judgment.

He declared that He would chastise them as their congregation had heard. The R.S.V. renders the last few words, "chastise them for their wicked deeds", but the literal wording is "chastise them according to the report to their congregation". The words presumably refer to the admonitions and warnings so often given to the nation by the prophets. As Jehovah had warned and the prophets had so clearly predicted, God's chastening hand would fall upon them.

EPHRAIM'S REBELLION

Woe to them for they wandered from me. Destruction to them because they rebelled against me. I indeed would redeem them, but they have spoken lies against me. They have not cried to me with their heart, but they howl on their beds. They cut themselves for corn and new wine, and they rebel against me. Though I indeed have trained and strengthened their arms, yet they devise mischief against me (Hos. 7 : 13–15).

With the deepest sorrow that His judgment should be necessary, Jehovah pronounced a woe upon Israel. They had wandered from Him. They had left their true home but had nowhere else to go. Destruction would be inflicted upon them because they had rebelled against Jehovah. Devastation was decreed because they had rejected His rule.

It had been Jehovah's intention to redeem His wayward people, but they had maligned Him by speaking falsehoods concerning Him. Ibn Ezra says that they erroneously thought that God was bent on destroying them. Their lies, in Cheyne's view, related to God's power and willingness to save them.

The Assyrian invasion of 733 B.C. had stripped the land and the people howled on their beds as they realised their loss. But Jehovah declared that they had not cried to Him from the heart. They merely treated Him as the equivalent of Baal. What they would have done in the Canaanite ritual, they actually performed. They cut themselves as did the followers of Baal (1 Kings 18 : 28), as though this self-mutilation would appeal to Jehovah. This action was forbidden by the law (Deut. 14 : 1), although it was habitually practised in the country.

Their concern was at the loss of the corn and the new wine and they presented their petition for help to Jehovah just as they presented their pleas to Baal. They regarded Jehovah as very little more than an alternative to Baal, and argued that He would be satisfied with the ritual of Baalism. God was not to be manipulated in this fashion and He declared that their idolatrous and apostate practices were a revolt against Himself. How could He answer their selfish supplications when they were in a state of rebellion against Him?

He had trained and strengthened their arms and made them strong to withstand the attack. Instead of displaying their gratitude by loyal submission to Him and recognition of His goodness to them, they devised mischief against Him. Their hearts were far away from Him and they had no true desire for Him. They were prepared to supplicate Him if there was any hope of recovering what they had lost—their prosperity and the productivity of the land—but this was sheer hypocrisy. In their continuing in the fertility cult rites, they were revolting against Jehovah.

DECEIT

They return, but not to the Most High. They are like a deceitful bow. Their princes shall fall by the sword because of the insolence of their tongue. This shall be their derision in the land of Egypt (Hos. 7 : 16).

There was a fictitious change of heart, declared Jehovah. They turned, in token of an intention to amend their ways, but they did not turn upward. There was no return to the Most High. There may have been a hypocritical show of repentance, but it was not sincere. Any apparent change of heart was unaccompanied by any evidence of a change of life and could, therefore, only be discounted. They returned, but not to the Most High. They turned, but not upward.

Scathingly, Hosea described them as a deceitful bow, one which shot its arrows in the wrong direction because of some defect in the bow. It was warped and, therefore, useless. McKeating (*The Books of Amos, Hosea and Micah* p. 118) says that "the compound bow in common use in the ancient Near East was a formidable and sophisticated weapon of laminated construction". If such a weapon failed the archer in the time of battle, it might be disastrous. It was a forceful image of Israel's dangerous unreliability. They could not be trusted.

The arrogant princes or leaders, who had virtually assumed responsibility for the destiny of the nation and who were consequently the cause of the vacillating diplomacy, would pay the price for their insolent murmuring against Jehovah. They considered themselves the best judges of the policy to be adopted and they wanted no relationship with God which would hinder their own intrigues. Their fate was pronounced bluntly and unequivocably: they would fall by the sword. The very fate, which they sought to avoid by their machinations, was the one which would befall them. Despite all their scheming, the land would be invaded by the Assyrians and they would die in battle. This, of course, actually occurred.

They would additionally suffer the mortification of being derided by Egypt, to whom they had boasted of Israel's strength, in the hope of enticing that country into an alliance with them. Their plans had gone completely awry and the day of reckoning had come: the penalty must be paid.

97

CHAPTER 9

The Imminent Invasion

ALTHOUGH the history of Assyria dated from the middle of the 18th century B.C., it rose to imperial power under Tiglath-pileser I (1114–1076 B.C.). Two centuries of retrogression were followed by the ruthless campaigns of Ashurnasirpal (883–859 B.C.) and his son Shalmaneser III (858–824 B.C.). In the 8th century B.C. Tiglath-pileser III (or Pul) conquered Babylon and overran Israel, taking tribute of Menahem and transporting many of the people to distant parts of the empire. After his death, Hoshea of Israel rebelled against Assyria, but Shalmaneser IV invaded the country and laid siege to Samaria, which eventually fell to Sargon II in 721 B.C. Jehu of Israel paid tribute to Shalmaneser III, and Menahem paid tribute to Tiglath-pileser III, but Pekah was defeated by the latter in 734 or 733 B.C. and it was probably to this invasion that Hosea now referred (2 Kings 15 : 29).

THE ALARM

Set the trumpet to your mouth, for one has come like a vulture against the house of Jehovah, because they have transgressed my covenant and rebelled against my law. To me they cry, My God (Elohim), we, Israel, know thee. Israel has cast off the good with loathing: the enemy shall pursue him (Hos. 8 : 1–3).

The threatened invasion was drawing nearer and the prophet was commanded to give warning of the approach of the enemy. Normally the watchman would give warning by a blast on the trumpet and the same figure was taken up and Hosea directed to set the trumpet to his mouth. His warning was predictive, but the event would not long be postponed. It was now imminent.

The enemy was likened to the carrion-eating griffon vulture renowned for its swiftness in swooping down on its prey (Job 9 : 26), a fitting symbol of the Assyrian forces, who were feared for the swiftness of their attack. The assault was described as against the house of Jehovah. This could not, of course, refer to the temple of Jerusalem, which was located in Judah, not Israel, but rather to the land of Israel as His house (cf. Hos. 9 : 15).

The reason for the impending invasion was clearly stated. It was because Israel had transgressed God's covenant or ordinance and had rebelled against His law. The people had been given every opportunity for repentance, but they had persisted in their course. They had dishonoured Jehovah and apostasised from Him, they had substituted the vile ceremonies of the fertility cult for the specific requirements of a Divinely given religion, they had ignored the Divine demands for sanctification and holy living, and in every conceivable way had done despite to God. Punishment could no longer be averted and they were to learn in exile the lesson they refused to learn in their own land.

When the people became aware of the imminence of the impending punishment, they turned hypocritically to Jehovah and cried, "My God, we, Israel, know Thee" (cf. Matt. 7 : 22). They had declined the knowledge of God and their cry now was sheer impertinence. It was only wrung from their lips because trouble was near and, in their folly, they thought to deliver themselves by stressing their relationship to Jehovah.

God was well aware of the superficiality of their apparent repentance and of the falsity of their plea. He declared that Israel had spurned the good—not casually or capriciously, but with loathing and complete distaste. How could they possibly now appeal to Jehovah? Their plea was rejected with the statement that the invasion was inevitable—"the enemy shall pursue him". They had rejected God so often when He had demonstrated His goodness to them that He could only dismiss their alleged recognition of Him and His relationship as insincere. We cannot deceive Him.

THE SCHISMATIC OFFENCE

They set up kings but not from me. They made princes but I knew it not. With their silver and their gold they made themselves idols, that they may be cut off (Hos. 8 : 4).

When the prophet Ahijah predicted the division of the kingdom, he specifically informed Jeroboam that Jehovah would award ten of the tribes of Israel to him and that he would be king over them (1 Kings 11 : 31–37). When Elisha anointed Jehu as king of Israel, he again explicitly stated that Jehovah had anointed him as such. On the other hand, the schism was not, of course, the original purpose of God and He has planned that one day the two kingdoms should be reunited (Ezek. 37 : 16–22).

The development of regal authority in Israel was quite independent of God. Men murdered and schemed to secure the throne without any recognition of the fact that power was derived from Him. They were not Divinely appointed and had no approval from Him. In the two and a half centuries of Israel's history as a separate kingdom, she had 17 kings, many of whom met a violent death. In the final period there was a rapid succession of usurpers of poor character, whom Jehovah did not recognise as legitimate. They did not reign by His will but as a result of intrigue and murder. The nation set up kings, He declared, but He did not acknowledge them. They made princes or rulers, but without His approval. As Horton (*op cit.*, p. 45) remarks, "It is the punishment of a nation destroyed by wine and whoredom that it has no man in the hour of its need, but only puppets, and no God but only idols".

100

Out of the gold and silver which the rulers amassed by dubious methods, they constructed idols for themselves, thus causing further dissension between the two kingdoms. The true temple of God was at Jerusalem, but Israel set apart its own shrines, and cast its golden calves as images of Jehovah. In the adoption of the Canaanite religion, they went farther and multitudes of images were made for the alleged protection of the country and the land. Figurines of all kinds have, in fact, been discovered in excavations.

These idolatrous images were another offence to Jehovah, since they were a denial of His authority and sufficiency and represented a filthy religion which was obnoxious to Him. Not only the idols themselves, but the people who trusted in them and used them in their rites and ceremonies of Baalism, had invoked the righteous anger of God and were destined to be destroyed.

SAMARIA'S CALF

Your calf, O Samaria, is loathsome. My anger burns against them. How long will they be incapable of innocency? For from Israel was this also: the workman made it: it is not God (Elohim). Samaria's calf shall be broken to pieces (Hos. 8 : 5, 6).

Jeroboam I placed golden calves at Bethel and Dan when he established official state sanctuaries there (1 Kings 12 : 26–33). It is possible that, when Samaria was built, another image was set up there, but there is no Scriptural confirmation of this. Ahab built a temple and altar for Baal at Samaria (1 Kings 16 : 32), but these and the statues of Baal were later destroyed by Jehu and the temple site converted into a latrine (2 Kings 10 : 26, 27). It has been suggested that Jeroboam's calves were merely pedestals in a bovine shape and that there was no idol surmounting them, but that the people subsequently identified the pedestals as images of the deity, but this is pure speculation.

Hosea identified the images of Bethel and Dan as Samaria's

101

calf. There is some dubiety about the significance of his words. The A.V. rendering says that the calf "has cast you off", but the R.S.V. translates it as "I have spurned your calf". G. A. Smith prefers "He loathes your calf", but Cheyne reverts to the intransitive sense and declares that the calf "is loathsome". This last is probably closer to the actual meaning. The idolatrous image, which virtually represented the religious life of the country, was repulsive to God. It robbed Him of His glory and degraded the Eternal to the level of the creatures He had made.

The Divine anger burned against the idolators. How long would it be before they could purge themselves from idolatry and free themselves from its taint? Would they ever be capable of attaining a state of purity again or was the evil too deeprooted? In the eyes of God, idolatry was an unclean thing, a defilement requiring cleaning. His people had contaminated themselves with unclean idols of the heathen.

This idol was Israel's work: it had no Divine sanction. It was the production of an artisan and could not, therefore, be regarded as a divine being; it was a deception, yet they worshipped the work of their hands. It was only made of wood and overlaid with gold or silver, according to the Talmud. Eventually it would be broken to pieces. Those who paid their adoration to this contemptible object deserved the derision of the prophet.

THE CONSEQUENCES

For they have sown the wind and they shall reap the whirlwind. It has no standing corn; the bud shall yield no meal; if so be it yield, strangers will swallow it up (Hos. 8 : 7).

The prophet showed the complete failure of Israel's policy, but they could not escape the consequences of their actions. The law of cause and effect operates inexorably. They would be faced by utter frustration. Hosea described them as sowing the wind and reaping the whirlwind. This was sheer futility. The wind was empty vanity, but the hurricane was a destructive force. If they committed folly, they would reap a harvest far more dreadful than any could have anticipated.

Hosea then depicted the nation as sowing corn, but finding that it never grew to full size, so that Israel had no standing corn. If it grew, it produced no grain. (In the Hebrew, there is another paronomasia, the *tsemach* will produce no *kemach*.) If all their toil resulted in the production of a small quantity of grain, even that would be lost: it would be devoured by aliens. It was a condemnation of the whole of their conduct and policy.

JUDGMENT PROCEEDS

Israel is swallowed up. Now they are among the nations as a vessel in which is no delight. For they have gone up to Assyria, a wild ass taking his own way by himself. Ephraim has hired lovers. Though they have hired among the nations, now will I gather them up, and they shall cease for a little while from anointing a king and princes (Hos. 8 : 8–10).

Israel was chosen from the nations of the earth to be a separate people, Jehovah's "peculiar treasure" (Exod. 19 : 5), but this meant nothing to them. Their mingling with the nations and their attempts to negotiate alliances with greater powers had robbed them of their peculiar identity. In due course—and the prophet regarded it as aready accomplished —they were swallowed up by the nations. After the Assyrian invasion in 733 B.C., for example, Galilee and Gilead were converted into Assyrian provinces and were no longer a part of Israel. They were gradually being absorbed.

Yet the nations treated them as a worthless vessel, something in which there was no pleasure to be found. Thomson (*The Land and the Book*, p. 36) says "The coarse pottery of this country is so cheap that even poor people throw it aside in contempt, or dash it to pieces on the slightest occasion". Israel was equally valueless in the eyes of the Gentiles.

Like a wild ass, obstinately choosing its own way and taking its own solitary course, Israel had turned to Assyria for help and strength. They were no better than Ishmael, who had been displaced by their ancestor: he was described as a wild ass (Gen. 16 : 12), but now they were described in the same way.

They had bribed the Assyrians to help them and Hosea caustically likened the gifts they sent Assyria to payments made by a prostitute to secure lovers. Normally the harlot would be the recipient of the payments, but the prophet declared that Israel was so unwanted that she had to pay to secure lovers. She had sunk to a new depth of degradation: she had to bribe her new allies heavily to secure their support and help.

By paying the nations, they had attempted to escape the judgment Jehovah had destined for them, but God announced that His purposes could not be thwarted thus: He would gather them up so that they could not escape. He intended their punishment by exile and this was now inescapable.

There is some doubt about the correct translation of the last clause of verse 10. The A.V. renders it, "they shall sorrow a little for the burden of the king of princes". Those who accept this translation see the title "king of princes" as that of Tiglath-pileser and the burden as the heavy tribute paid to him. It is possible, however, that the meaning is rather that there would be a respite before any more rulers were hastily chosen. This is also in line with the Septuagint version.

There is no doubt that the purchasing of allies was a heavy financial burden for Israel. Their negotiations were expensive. And since they belonged to Jehovah, there was no need for other help. Yet they relied on man rather than God.

RELIGIOUS FAILURE

Because Ephraim has multiplied altars for sinning, they have become to him altars for sinning. I have written for him the multitude of precepts of my law, but they are counted as a strange thing. They sacrifice flesh for the sacrifices of my offerings and eat it. But Jehovah does not accept them. Now will he remember their iniquity and punish their sins. They shall return to Egypt (Hos. 8 : 11–13).

104

The threatened judgment found justification in Israel's religious activities as well as in their political intrigues. The establishment of religious sanctuaries, followed by the adoption of the fertility cult, resulted in a multiplication of altars. The erection of these was, of course, initially for the purpose of propitiating God: they existed—at least in the minds of the worshippers—for the presentation of offerings and sacrifices to atone for sins and to remove the offerer's sense of guilt. But the proliferation of altars to deal with the question of sin had a totally different effect. The altars became associated with the immoral ritual of the false deities and, instead of being places for the expiation of sin, became sites for the committing of sin.

If the altars had been multiplied, Jehovah stated that He had multiplied the revelations of His will. The ethical precepts of the *torah* had been set down in writing and, in Hosea's time, the written law was quite voluminous. The reference was not, of course, merely to the ceremonial law, but also to the judicial law.

Astonishingly, the prophet declared that Israel had treated these written statements of the Divine requirements as a strange thing, as the will of an alien deity unknown to them. They deliberately rejected the ethical and spiritual precepts entrusted to them and accounted them as strange and irrelevant to the circumstances of life.

In most pagan religions, sacrifice was followed by a feast upon the flesh of the animal offered to the deity. Since part of the offering was consumed upon the altar and became symbolically the food of the god or goddess, the worshipper's act of feeding upon some of the flesh was an indication of communion with the god. The deity and the offerer participated in the same meal. The same concept was found, for example, in the peace offering (Lev. 3) of the Levitical system: Jehovah fed upon that part of the animal consumed by fire upon the altar (His table), while the worshipper also feasted upon part of the same animal. Figuratively, fellowship was thereby established between Jehovah and the worshipper.

Hosea accused the people of being more concerned with their share of the offering than with their sacrificial gift to Jehovah. They delighted in presenting their sacrifices, but only because of the feast which they subsequently enjoyed. This was of no moral or spiritual value. God saw the unreality of their hearts. The offerer was identified with the offering: if it was accepted, he found acceptance before God: if it was rejected, then he was also rejected. Jehovah declared that He did not accept them. Their sacrifices were unavailing: they were the gifts of insincere hearts, and God rejected them.

Since God was not prepared to accept their sin and trespass offerings, their iniquity was unforgiven and their sins were not atoned for. Their guilt must, therefore, be judicially dealt with, and Jehovah declared that He would remember (or bring under review) their iniquity and would punish their sins. There was no alternative. Hypocrisy and insincerity were to bear their fruit. He would demonstrate that He had not overlooked their transgressions.

The nation had been redeemed from Egypt. The punishment to be imposed was that they should return thereto. In Egypt they had known oppression and hardship, bondage and sorrow. By implication, there was to be a return to the same conditions. When Hoshea's kingdom finally fell to the Assyrians, the majority of the people were deported to Assyria, but some did, in fact, flee to Egypt, thereby reversing the history of the past. There seems no need to assume, however, that the prediction was restricted to Egypt. That country was regarded as "the house of bondage" and the use of the name was probably intended metaphorically rather than literally. It could, therefore, cover the Assyrian captivity and possible future experiences of the nation.

INDEPENDENCE

For Israel has forgotten his Maker and builds palaces; and Judah has multiplied fortified cities; but I will send a fire upon his cities and it shall devour their castles (Hos. 8 : 14).

106

One of the greatest tragedies was that Israel had forgotten their Maker. He was their salvation and security and all that they needed was discoverable in Him. Yet they ignored Jehovah as though he did not exist and sought to create their own means of defence.

They built palaces, which may imply either royal residences or temples—in the latter case, for the false gods. Even Judah had developed an extensive defence programme and had built fortified cities in strategic sites (2 Kings 18 : 13). Both kingdoms relied upon their own strength, their planning and their ingenuity to deliver them in the day of trouble.

But Jehovah declared that He would send fire upon the cities which would destroy the strongholds,. The very defences upon which they relied would be swept away.

CHAPTER 10

Joy Dispelled

THE Feast of Tabernacles (*Succoth*) was a week of rejoicing held in the autumn when the harvest had been
gathered in. It was the custom to dwell in rude "booths"
made of tree branches, as a reminder of the dwellings in which
the people lived after the exodus from Egypt. Offerings were
brought to God each day in token of gratitude for the harvest
and the whole festival was one in which the rejoicing was before Him (Lev. 23, 34-44). The next section of the prophecy
was set in the framework of the festival.

MISPLACED JOY

*Rejoice not, O Israel, unto exultation like the peoples: for
you have gone a-whoring from your God (Elohim). You have
loved a harlot's hire upon all threshing floors. The threshing
floor and the wine vat shall not feed them and the new wine
shall fail her (Hos. 9 : 1, 2).*

The celebration of the festival was evidently being con-
ducted with an unparalleled exuberance and possibly in
emulation of the orgies and excesses of the heathen. This was
not the character of the Divinely appointed festival, which was
a holy convocation to Jehovah. Joy had a place in that,
but the unrestrained exultation and wild shouting, in which
the people were apparently indulging, was quite foreign to
the original conception of Tabernacles.

108

Hosea called upon the people to cease their imitation of the pagans and to curb their uncontrolled demonstrations. This was not Jehovah's feast: they were not bringing their thanksgivings to Him. Bluntly he declared that they had played the whore and had virtually turned their back upon Jehovah. Instead of attributing the blessings of harvest to Jehovah, they ascribed them to Baal. It was to Baal they brought their firstfruits and in his honour that they indulged in the rites of the nature worship. They had broken their marriage bond with Jehovah and had become a whore.

The wild revelling on every threshing-floor and in the oil-presses and wine vats did not spring from an appreciation of the goodness of God. In the words of the prophet, they had "loved a harlot's hire upon all threshing floors". As a whore was bound to her paramour by the "hire" he paid for her services, so Israel was bound to the false deities of Baalism. There may have been a subtle reminder in Hosea's words, not only of the offerings made to the idol gods, but to the licentious practices required by the nature worship. Had they not committed adultery with the temple prostitutes on every threshing floor? Idolatrous Israel, in his eyes, was herself nothing but a whore.

They had abused the blessings of God and now He intended judicially to remove them. In future the threshing floor would not provide food for them: in other words, because of their sin, the next harvest would fail. They had drunk the new wine in the feasts of their idolatrous worship, but it would be lacking when they looked to it to satisfy their desires. They had virtually blasphemed Him in attributing the gifts of His hand to the pagan Baal. Let Baal supply their need: since he was impotent, they would be taught that only in Jehovah was their satisfaction. Their sin could no longer be tolerated and they must now pay the price for their infidelity.

THE EXPULSION

They shall not dwell in Jehovah's land; but Ephraim shall

return to Egypt, and they shall eat unclean food in Assyria. They shall not pour out wine to Jehovah, neither shall their sacrifices be pleasing to him. Their bread shall be to them as the bread of mourning; all who eat of it shall be polluted; for their bread shall be only for their hunger; it shall not come into the house of Jehovah (Hos. 9 : 3, 4).

The land of Israel was Jehovah's property (Lev. 25 : 23) and He could not tolerate the presence therein of a rebellious and idolatrous people. If His ultimate plan was to be achieved, they must be purged of their sin and idolatry and taught to recognise Him as their true benefactor. It was necessary, therefore, to deprive them of their material blessings and possessions and to remove them from everything in which they trusted, and this was His stated intention.

No longer would they be permitted to dwell in His land. There they defiled the land and themselves by the false system of worship. They would be removed therefrom. Once more He declared that Ephraim should return to Egypt—a threat, one writer says, "well calculated to deter the Israelites from disobedience." Egypt stood metaphorically for exile and captivity, for the rigours of slavery and all the hardships of bondage. These were to be experienced once more by the nation, although not necessarily in the land of the south.

In confirmation of this, He intimated that they would eat unclean food in Assyria. They had had the opportunity of enjoying "clean" food in the holy land. In view of their behaviour, they would eat food in a foreign land which had not been sanctified by the offering of part of the food to Jehovah. Indeed, they might be forced to eat food, part of which had been offered to the false deities of the land of their exile, and they would be defiled thereby.

They had defrauded Jehovah of His due. Now they would be unable to pour out libations of wine to Him as required by the law. These accompanied the burnt offerings, meal offerings and peace offerings (Num. 15 : 1–11). There would be no sanctuary in a foreign land at which they could acceptably

110

worship God or offer their sacrifices to Him. Defiled and out of communion with Him, no sacrifice they could bring would be acceptable to Him. They had despised the worship of Jehovah and the religion of their fathers. Now they were to be deprived of it.

Their food and wine would be unsanctified and they would accordingly be defiled in partaking of it. If they ate, it would be merely to satisfy their hunger, but their food was no more attractive than the bread of mourners. Lehrman (op. cit., p. 33) says, "To this day Jewish mourners, returning home from a funeral, partake of a meal prepared for them by friends, doubtless a reminder of the fact that food kept in the house while the corpse was unburied becomes virtually unclean." There would be no pleasure for the exiles in their meals: no joyous feasts would be theirs. The happiness of those, who had paid their tithes and who presented their first-lings and their sacrifices to God, was denied them. There could be no joy, therefore, in eating the food which was virtually unblessed. It was only by this means that God could teach them the enormity of their transgression and the value of the true religion which they had despised. There was no idolatry after the return from exile.

NO FEASTS

What will you do on the day of assembly and on the day of the feast of Jehovah? (Hos. 9:5).

Even after the schism, Jeroboam I ensured that festivals were held at the same time as those appointed by the law and these were celebrated in similar fashion in honour of Jehovah The tendency to travel to Jerusalem on the festival occasions was thereby arrested. But when the nation was carried into captivity into Assyria or "Egypt", it would be impossible to celebrate the feasts. The day of assembly, or the day appointed for the festival, and the day on which Jehovah's feast was to be held would be a torment instead of a joy.

The religious calendar no longer had any significance. It

was but a constant reminder of what might have been, and a cause for despondency and despair because of the people's very inability to carry out the observance. No longer could the rejoicing of the festivals be their experience, and no more could they recover their peace of mind by the annual fast or by daily sacrifices. "What will you do?" asked the prophet. Life would be void of spiritual satisfaction.

DAYS OF VISITATION

For behold, they are going from the devastation. Egypt shall gather them up, Memphis shall bury them. Nettles shall possess their precious things of silver; thorns shall be in their tents. The days of visitation have come, the days of recompense have come. Israel shall know. The prophet is a fool, the spiritual man is mad, for the greatness of your iniquity and because the enmity is great (Hos. 9 : 6, 7).

In the Spirit, Hosea saw the blow fall. The day of punishment had come and the horrors of the Assyrian invasion were being experienced to the full. Those to whom his words were addressed must have ridiculed them. They had bought off Assyria and feared no danger from that quarter. Yet, speaking prophetically, Hosea described the scene when the invader had overrun the country.

Many of the survivors, he saw fleeing from the devastated land, seeking a refuge in Egypt. But they would find no shelter there. It would be an escape from Israel to death in Egypt. There they would be gathered together for burial. At Memphis, the capital of Egypt, the area of pyramids and mausoleums even at that date, they would be buried. Their hope of salvation was doomed to disappointment. The necropolis of Memphis stretches for 20 miles, a reminder of the prophet's prediction.

Nettles would overgrow their treasure cities, said Hosea, so that their precious things of silver, including the images of the idols, would be swallowed up. If his address was delivered— as seems probable—during the feast of tabernacles, his words

112

were ironical, for he declared that thorns would be in their tabernacles or tents. Their cities and villages would be lost in weeds, thorns and thistles. Proud Israel would be utterly humiliated and subjected to the utmost discomfort.

The days of punishment and requital had come. Jehovah had long delayed in mercy, but ultimately the recompense was meted out. The ruthlessness of the conquerors would be demonstrated in their brutality and harsh treatment of the conquered. All this came to pass precisely as foretold by Hosea, and Israel suffered for her sins. Israel would then know by experience (Isa. 9 : 9).

Yet the people to whom he had been sent only slandered him. "The prophet is a fool," they cried, "the man of spirit is mad." Hosea's utterances must clearly have aroused considerable antagonism, and the reproach was bitter. He had denounced people, king and rulers, and had torn aside the veil of hypocrisy and insincerity and revealed the people for what they really were. It was not surprising that opposition was aroused. Whether active enmity eventuated we do not know: the historical record gives no clue.

The slander uttered by Israel was indicative of the magnitude of the nation's iniquity, said the prophet, and also of the great enmity felt towards him because of his public statements. Their hostility was thoroughly aroused because of his attacks upon them.

THE WATCHMAN

The watchman of Ephraim is with my God (Elohim). The prophet is a fowler's snare in all his ways, and enmity in the house of his God (Elohim) (Hos. 9 : 8).

This verse presents some problems in translation. The A.V. (which is largely followed above) virtually identifies the watchman with the prophet. The R.S.V. renders, "The prophet is the watchman of Ephraim, the people of my God . . .", but Lehrman translates, "Ephraim is a watchman with my God", and G. A. Smith follows this. It can hardly be maintained that Ephraim was a watchman with God, and there can be little doubt that the watchman must be identified with Hosea (cf. Jer. 6 : 17; Hab. 2 : 1).

Hosea claimed by implication that his words were reliable and that his predictions would be fulfilled, since he stood on the watchtower with God and could see into the distance as the normal watchman would. It is possible that the fowler's snare referred to the traps constantly set in the prophet's way by the people. The R.S.V. renders the next clause, "yet a fowler's snare is on all his ways", and this conforms with a number of other versions. If this view is adopted, the implication is that the people treated the prophet as no better than a wild beast to be entrapped and destroyed. His path was strewn with traps to ensnare him. The "enmity in the house of God" (i.e., in the land itself) would then relate to Israel's hatred of Jehovah and His servant.

EVIL CONDUCT

They have deeply corrupted themselves, as in the days of Gibeah. He will remember their iniquity, he will punish their sins (Hos. 9 : 9).

The prophet scathingly compared the people's treatment of him with the atrocity at Gibeah centuries earlier. He declared that they had deeply corrupted themselves. It may be that he referred incidentally to the immorality and cruelty of Israel as a parallel of that of the Benjamites (Jud. 19:22-30), and tacitly warned them of the fate of the latter, who were all destroyed but 600 (Jud. 20:46-48). Jehovah did not ignore the sin of centuries earlier, and Hosea declared that He would remember the iniquity of Israel and punish their sins. He would not forget.

EARLY SIN

I found Israel like grapes in the wilderness. I saw your fathers as the first ripe on the fig-tree at her first time. But

114

they went to Baal-peor and consecrated themselves to shame, and became abominations like that which they loved (Hos. 9 : 10).

Israel's unfaithfulness to God was not of recent origin: it dated back to the earliest days of their relationship. Jehovah recalled the delight which He first found in His people. In an unusual simile He said that He found them as grapes in the wilderness. The vine is normally a cultivated plant and it is not usually found in the wild places of the wilderness. The pleasure of discovering grapes in such a place would naturally be enhanced by the unlikelihood. He found a joy in His people then.

He saw their fathers, He added, as the first ripe fruit on the fig tree at the moment when ripening commenced. The early white fig ripens between April and June—at least two months before the black fig. Many describe it as the sweetest of all fruit. The similes were expressive of the delight which Jehovah found in Israel.

Yet they departed early from Him. Almost plaintively He referred to their unfaithfulness. They went to Baal-peor and consecrated themselves to shame (*bamoth*) and became like the object of their devotion. It was at Baal-peor that Baalam's machinations succeeded (Num. 25 : 1–9). Having failed in his attempts to curse the people of God, he finally proposed their seduction by heathen women. The people fell and not only committed adultery with the Moabite women but apparently commenced practising the rites and ceremonies of the nature worship of Baalism.

Idolatry—and particularly Baalism—was frequently referred to detrimentally as *bamoth* or shame, and Jehovah declared that, at Baal-peor, they had consecrated themselves to shame. Moreover, He added that they became abominations like that which they loved. The character of the idols was impressed upon them. It is frequently said that we grow like the objects of our love. They had devoted themselves to the pagan deities and, in their polluted practices, had assumed the same character. The word "abomination" is used in the Old Testament almost as a synonym for "idol" and "idolatry". They were idolaters and, therefore, abominations.

Ephraim's glory shall fly away like birds: there shall be no birth, no pregnancy, no conception. Though they bring up children, I will bereave them till none is left. Woe to them when I look away from them (Hos. 9 : 11, 12).

Because of the nation's sin, Hosea graphically portrayed their prosperity as taking wings to itself and flying away like birds. Material prosperity was the indication of Divine blessing under the old economy, just as spiritual prosperity is the sign of God's blessing in the Christian era. Some expositors restrict the word "glory" to the children but, although they were regarded as part of a man's prosperity, the concept went much farther. Some also interpret the "glory" as the realisation of God's presence and suggest that the moral obliquity of the people resulted in the loss of communion with Him.

At Baal-peor the people had indulged in immorality and adulterous rites. In Hosea's day this had been repeated on an even more extensive scale, and the moral defilement and spiritual decay of Israel demanded fit retribution. The punishment was certainly appropriate to their sins against chastity: there would be no birth, pregnancy or conception. Miscarriage and sterility would be the curse to fall upon them. Since children were considered one of life's greatest blessings and the gift of God's hands, the blow was an extremely serious one.

Israel could not take comfort in the children already conceived or born, for God declared that, even if children survived birth and infancy, they would not be permitted to become adults. He would bereave the parents of all their progeny and none would be left. There would be none to carry on a father's name and none to comfort the widowed

116

mother in her hour of trial. By famine, disease, pestilence, war and deportation, families would be destroyed.

"Woe to them when I look away from them," said Jehovah. Their sorrow was not complete with the loss of children, for they were to lose their God as well. J. L. Mays (*Hosea*, p. 134) says, "He will abdicate His place as their God, and their ultimate extremity shall be the silent, vacant emptiness above and around them." Nothing could be more awful. Their depravity was such that the Almighty withdrew from them, leaving them to plunge into irremedial ruin.

EPHRAIM'S FATE

Ephraim, as I saw Tyre, is planted in a pleasant place. But Ephraim shall bring forth his children to the murderer. Give them, O Jehovah: what wilt thou give? Give them a miscarrying womb and dry breasts (Hos. 9 : 13, 14).

Verse 13 has created difficulties in translation for many writers. The R.S.V., following the Septuagint, reads, "Ephraim's sons, as I have seen, are destined for a prey. Ephraim must lead forth his sons to slaughter." George Adam Smith renders very similarly. The Peshitta translates, "Ephraim's fate shall be like that of Tyre, as you have seen, though planted in a pleasant place with buildings. Likewise Ephraim shall bring out his children to the slaughter."

Tyre, once a wealthy prosperous city, was reduced to ruins (Isa. 23). Ephraim was to suffer the same fate, although it had been located in a pleasant place. Jehovah had intended that a glory, comparable with that of Tyre, should be bestowed upon His people. But their apostasy and infidelity doomed it to destruction, and that fate was now impending.

Verse 14 reads superficially as a petition on behalf of Israel, but the second half of the verse makes it clear that the oracle was intended as a curse. As a patriot, Hosea first begged Jehovah to give to His people, but in perplexity and not knowing what was best, he cried, "What wilt Thou give?" Ewald terms his cry "a paroxysm of despair. Finally he decided that

117

It was better for a woman to be childless than to bring children into such a world."

Therefore, he prayed Jehovah to give them a miscarrying womb and dry breasts. Barrenness was preferable to the loss of the young at an age when they were emerging into full growth.

NO LOVE

All their wickedness is in Gilgal: for there I hated them. Because of the wickedness of their deeds, I will drive them out of my house. I will love them no more: all their princes are rebels. Ephraim is stricken. Their root is dried up, they shall bear no fruit. Even though they bring forth, I will slay the beloved fruit of their womb (Hos. 9 : 15, 16).

Gilgal was one of the principal centres of the idolatrous worship of the northern kingdom. It was here that Israel, like an adulterous wife, proved unfaithful to Jehovah. Here she turned her back upon Him and resorted to the Baalim. Here the people indulged in the immoral rites of the fertility cult. Justifiably God declared that all their wickedness had its focus there.

It was there that He learned to hate them, i.e., to prefer them less. Their sinfulness had defiled them and they were no longer fit to be united to Him. He hated the wickedness of their deeds and He was compelled to drive His adulterous wife out of His house, i.e., out of the land of Israel. This would be effected by the Assyrian deportation.

He would love them no more. Surely this, above all else, should have brought Israel to a realisation of the nation's sin. They had been the object of His love and compassion, but now His affection was to be withdrawn from them.

All their princes or leaders were rebels. These were the men who, in submission to the Divine will, should have directed the nation into paths in conformity to that will. But they had all revolted against Jehovah and were transgressors like all the rest. It was a tragic situation.

118

Ephraim should have been a fruitful tree, but the tree had been smitten by heat, drought or lightning. Root and branches had dried up and there was consequently no fruit. Using the same figure in relation to the individuals, He announced that if any bore children, He would destroy "the beloved fruit" —not of the tree but of the womb. They should bear no fruit. They were under the curse of God.

CAST AWAY

My God (Elohim) will cast them away, because they have not hearkened to him: and they shall be fugitives among the nations (Hos. 9 : 17).

It is significant that Hosea referred to his God and, by implication, indicated the temporary cessation of the Divine relationship with Israel. Ephraim had been rejected and now the prophet declared that God had decided to cast them away because they had not hearkened to Him. Despite all His pleas, they had ignored Him. Now they were to become homeless refugees among the nations.

This prediction was literally fulfilled. After the fall of Samaria in 721 B.C., the inhabitants of the northern kingdom were removed from the land and dispersed to all parts of the Assyrian empire and scattered so completely that they were ultimately swallowed up in the nations and lost their identity. Their fate was well deserved.

Horton (*op. cit.*, p. 53) says that Hosea "was the first to trace the connection between sexual immorality and national decay. It is Hosea too who first by his preaching of repentance showed that there was redemption even from this most insidious and corrupting of vices." It was Hosea also who indicated the inescapable penalty for the one who persisted in his sin.

CHAPTER 11

Israel's Guilt

HOSEA had indicated the inevitability of the Divine judgment on Israel and had disclosed the fate of the people when the blow ultimately fell. He now proceeded to examine still further the nation's guilt and the consequent punishment she must experience.

FRUIT FOR SELF

Israel is a luxuriant vine, which puts forth fruit freely. As his fruit increased, he increased his altars. The better it was with his land, the better he made his pillars (Hos. 10 : 1).

Israel had been given the fruitful land of Canaan and had been planted therein as a vine by Jehovah. Every blessing had been showered upon it and God might reasonably have anticipated that the vine of His planting would bear fruit to Him. Instead, it had grown luxuriantly and had produced an abundance of fruit, but not for God: the proceeds had been directed to another object.

When they had taken the land of Canaan, Israel also adopted the pagan religion. Material prosperity was employed only to further the interests of that religion. As the fruit increased, as the people became more prosperous, so they built more altars to the false gods of the land instead of devoting their substance to Jehovah, from whom their prosperity was derived. Their material wealth only served to extend the influence of the idolatrous system.

They developed a penchant for building and embellishing the instruments of Baal. As their affluence increased, so they improved the *mazzeboth* or pillars erected by Baal's altars, possibly decorating them or overlaying them with precious metal. Ignoring the gifts of Jehovah, they ascribed their well-being to Baal, and the homage and material gifts which should have been presented to Jehovah were offered to Baal.

A DECEITFUL RACE

Their heart is false; now must they be dealt with as guilty. He shall break the neck of their altars. He shall destroy their pillars. For now they will say, We have no king because we feared not Jehovah. What could a king do for us? (Hos. 10 : 2, 3).

Israel was trying to worship both Jehovah and Baal, who were mutually exclusive. Their devotion was divided between the two, because they were afraid to risk breaking with either. Their heart was really false or deceitful (one version renders it "slippery"). They were not faithful to Jehovah, for they maintained that the corn, wine and oil were produced because of the fertility rites in which they engaged, instead of recognising that they were the bountiful gifts of God's hand.

They were guilty and must be dealt with as such. God accordingly declared that He would break the necks of their altars. He would strike off the horns of the altars and thereby destroy their efficacy, since the sacrifices must be fastened to the horns. Some expositors have suggested that images of calves, or heads of calves, were placed on the corners of the altars and that it was these which were struck off: it is more likely, however, that the reference was to the usual horns of the altars.

God also declared that He would destroy the *mazzeboth* or pillars. Originally dedicated to Him, these pillars were normally associated with the worship of Baal, and it was appropriate that their destruction should occur together with that of the altars.

They had virtually rejected Jehovah as their God and also as their Supreme Ruler. They had set up kings on their own authority, but were conscious of the unworthiness of their puppets. Now they lamented that they had no king to rule over them. The words may, of course, have been spoken after the assassination of Pekah, when they actually had no sovereign. But it is probable that the statement was more general and implied that the monarchy had become an empty symbol, thoroughly discredited as a political or administrative force.

They had abandoned Jehovah and acknowledged that the absence of rule was attributable to this. Even if they had a king, what could he do for them? they asked. He was virtually powerless as ruler, judge, military leader or head of government. Such a ruler was of no value to any kingdom.

FALSE COVENANTS

They have spoken words: they swear falsely in making covenants. So judgment springs up like the poppy in the furrows of the field (Hos. 10 : 4).

Turning to the political sphere once more, the prophet accused them of merely uttering words, unaccompanied by effectual deeds. They used words in swearing falsely as they solemnly entered into treaties with Egypt and Assyria. They were deceitful in their political negotiations and had no intention of fulfilling their covenanted obligations if they could be avoided. McKeating and others identify the covenants referred to with those entered into by the king at his coronation, and repeated annually, in which he pledged himself to uphold justice and to serve God and the people. The pledges were nothing but empty words in the prophet's view. They were never implemented and had no real significance. This is a possible interpretation, but it seems more probable that Hosea had in view the relations with other nations.

122

Their wrongdoing attracted judgment and Hosea depicted it springing up swiftly as the poppy suddenly appears in the furrows of the field. The poppy cannot be identified with certainty. It was said to be an umbelliferous plant, commonly known as *rosh*. or "head", and described as bitter (Deut. 29 : 18). It grew abundantly in Palestine. The poisonous hemlock also grew profusely and the A.V. adopts this as the appropriate term.

CAPTURED GODS

The inhabitants of Samaria shall tremble for the calves of Bethaven. Its people shall mourn for it and its priests shall tremble for it, for its glory because it has gone into exile from them. This also shall be carried to Assyria as a present to the contentious king. Ephraim shall be put to shame, and Israel shall be ashamed through his own counsel (Hos. 10 : 5, 6).

The judgment which was to spring up so swiftly was, of course, that of which Hosea had already so frequently spoken, viz., the invasion of the Assyrians and all the trials which ensued. In their hour of calamity the people might justifiably be expected to turn to their gods for help. Since they had rejected Jehovah, the idols were the only alternative. But ironically the prophet recorded that, far from discovering help in these, the people were fearful for the welfare of their gods.

It was a ludicrous situation. The inhabitants of Samaria brought their homage to the golden calves at the shrines established by Jeroboam. But these images were now in danger from the invader and the people were concerned to know how to protect their deity. They trembled at the possibility of the images of Bethaven being destroyed or captured. They had trusted in them for security: where could they turn if these were carried off?

As they realised the inevitability of what they feared, they mourned for the deity. The priests (*kemarim*) of the false religion also trembled. These ministers of paganism would lose their honour and their service if the images were lost. To their horror, they saw the Assyrians seize and remove the idols. The gods were being exiled from their own land. Moreover, the idols were being carried to Assyria as a present to the king. The A.V. translates the latter as "king Jareb", but there is no record of a king of that name in history. Presumably it was the warlike ruler or contentious king of Assyria who was intended.

The images gone and the shrine empty, the nation was exposed to shame: they had worshipped a powerless deity who was incapable of defending or protecting himself. It was customary for a victor to carry off the gods of a conquered land, to demonstrate the superiority of his own gods, but the further indignity was usually added that the metal (often gold or silver) of which they were composed was then added to the treasures of the war. Israel was disgraced through their own decision to pay homage to an inanimate object and to trust in a non-existent deity. The stupidity was evident.

END OF AUTHORITY

Samaria's king shall perish like a chip on the face of the waters. The high places also of Aven, the sin of Israel, shall be destroyed; the thorn and the thistle shall grow up on their altars: and they shall say to the mountains, Cover us, and to the hills, Fall on us (Hos. 10 : 7, 8).

The invasion so vividly predicted by Hosea had widespread effects. It meant the end of the monarchy and of the idolatrous system of religion. Royal and religious authority were broken. Samaria's king (not a particular ruler but the monarchy itself), he declared, would perish like a chip of wood carried away by a torrent, tossed helplessly hither and thither as a useless thing. It could not survive and this, in fact, proved to be so in history. The deportation of the people and the overrunning of the country meant the end of Israel's rule.

The local sanctuaries, or high places of the calf-worship, were also destroyed. The images gone, there would be no point in retaining the shrines or in observing the rites and ceremonies. Aven probably stood for the whole of the sanctuaries scattered throughout the land. This was described as the sin of Israel, as though it was beyond all other iniquity. It had started with the misrepresentation of Jehovah and had then become a substitute for Him. There could be no greater crime.

Thorns and thistles would grow up on the altars and eventually the shrines would be completely covered from view. The curse originally pronounced upon the ground (Gen. 3 : 18) now embraced the sites of the idolatrous religion and obliterated them completely.

Deprived of all help and protection, both from the royal court and the rulers of the country and from the false deities they had served, the people would cry out in terror in their extremity. There was no protection from judgment and Jehovah had turned His face from them. In anguished fear, they would seek any refuge or even prefer sudden death to protracted shame. The prophet predicted that they would implore the mountains to cover them and the hills to fall upon them, but all to no avail.

As the New Testament indicates, in a future day others will similarly cry out for shelter and to be hidden from the eyes of the Eternal Judge, but their cry will be equally unavailing (Luke 23 : 30; Rev. 6 : 16). There may be a reference to this later fulfilment in the prophecy, as well as to the more imminent one.

GIBEAH'S SIN

O Israel, you have sinned from the days of Gibeah. There they stood that the battle against the sons of iniquity might not overtake them in Gibeah (Hos. 10 : 9).

If Israel was to be punished so drastically, it was because of their sin, and the prophet accused them of consistently following the path of wrongdoing. They had sinned from the days of Gibeah. Jewish commentators usually connect this

125

verse with the shameful incident of the violated concubine at Gibeah and then the sanguinary battle which resulted therefrom (Jud. 19, 20). Israel's conduct had been equally heinous and the immorality of her religion was equally blameworthy. Her depravity was comparable with the outrage and summary vengeance of Gibeah. It has also been suggested—although with less justification perhaps—that the prophet may also have had in mind the people's rejection of Jehovah and the crowning of Saul of Gibeah (1 Sam. 10 : 19).

The stand against the battle at Gibeah can only refer to the incident in the days of the Judges. Cheyne (*op. cit.*, p. 104) pertinently comments, "Just as the Benjamites offered a stubborn resistance to the onset of the rest of Israel at Gibeah, so the Israelites persist in their old iniquities, and defy Jehovah to put them down."

GOD'S INTENTION

When I desire, I will chastise them; and peoples shall be gathered against them, when I chastise them for their two iniquities (Hos. 10 : 10).

"Israel as a people," says one writer, "took summary vengeance on the Benjamites for the outrage of Gibeah. But the seed of wickedness remained and developed into evil practices worthy only of the Gibeah of old." Because of this, punishment was essential. It was the inevitable concomitant of wrongdoing. It would be inflicted at the appointed time. When Jehovah decided that the time had come, He would chastise Israel.

The instruments of castigation would be the nations to whom they had looked for help. These would be gathered together against them. Mays (*op. cit.*, p. 144) writes, "The old amphictyonic process for maintaining covenant order has been translated into the process of world history in order to chastise Israel for breach of covenant." As the supreme lord of world history, Jehovah used the nations as He pleased to

126

work out His purposes and, in this instance, for the disciplining of his wayward people.

By these instruments, i.e., the hostile armies of their heathen neighbours, Jehovah announced that He would chastise Israel for their two iniquities. The A.V. reads, "when they shall bind themselves in their two furrows", but there is no support for the translation "furrows" and the clause as thus rendered is quite unintelligible. The sense seems to be as proposed above. Lehrman renders the latter part of the verse, "I will have Judah and Ephraim ploughed together. Their sorrows and trials will be doubled"; but this is interpretation rather than translation.

The two iniquities or transgressions for which chastisement was to be inflicted have been variously interpreted. The most obvious are either the attempt to serve Jehovah and Baal, or the moral and religious failure of the nation; but it may possibly refer to the rejection of God and the disinclination to observe the rule of temporal authority. There is the further possibility of the reference being to the two forms of idolatry adopted by the people—the golden calves on the one hand and the Baalim on the other. Even if the specific significance is not clear, it is plain that the punishment was for particular attitudes and transgressions.

THE HEIFER'S WORK

Ephraim is a heifer broken in and loving to thresh, and I have spared the beauty of her neck; but now will I make Ephraim to be ridden. Judah shall plough; Jacob shall break his clods (Hos. 10 : 11).

Still continuing the subject of Israel's punishment, the prophet next described it as a means of training, and contrasted the former prosperity of the nation with the hardships they were soon to experience. Ephraim, said Hosea, was a heifer which had been broken in and taught to thresh corn by walking round and round, treading out the corn. This was an easy and pleasant task and, since the animal was not muzzled, it was free to eat as it worked (Deut. 25 : 4). Such labour was congenial and was typical of Israel's lot in days of prosperity.

But sooner or later the owner of such a draught animal would place it on harder work, which would involve the yoke, which chafed the neck. Ploughing and harrowing might be less pleasant labour, but the discipline of such work had also to be learned. When Israel had been treated with every consideration, she had turned away from her Master and had abused His kindness. In consequence, He decided to put her to the heavy labour of the fields. In captivity the nation would learn hardships and rigours which she had never previously experienced, and suffer wounds from which she had hitherto preserved. Chastisement was, therefore, necessary, not only as a punishment for wrongdoing, but also as part of the discipline required in training.

Judah also had transgressed in similar fashion and must eventually suffer in the same way. She should plough and Jacob (as typical of the whole nation) should break up the heavy clods of earth. The Divine purposes were for the ultimate good and blessing of both nations.

THE PROPHET'S APPEAL

Sow to yourselves righteousness and reap lovingkindness. Break up your fallow ground; for it is time to seek Jehovah that he may come and rain salvation upon you. You have ploughed wickedness and reaped injustice. You have eaten the fruit of lies, because you have trusted in your chariots and in the multitude of your warriors (Hos. 10 : 12, 13).

Hosea seemed convinced that the judgment he had predicted could even yet be averted if true repentance took place. Therefore, he pleaded with the people to change their conduct. "Sow to yourselves righteousness," he said, "and reap lovingkindness." If they amended their ways and practised righteousness and made right living their aim, then the harvest they would reap would not be the calamities he had foretold, but lovingkindness or mercy. It was not too late to produce

128

the fruits of repentance. If they did, mercy would respond to their change of attitude.

The seeds of righteousness could not be sown in hard hearts though, and he bade them to break up their fallow ground. The heavy clods must be broken up and the ground ploughed and harrowed. The habits which they had cultivated and the behaviour patterns which they had formed must be transformed. The hard heart must feel the crushing and the breaking of the Holy Spirit, but this could only be with their own concurrence.

The matter was urgent. It was time to seek Jehovah and He would come and rain salvation upon them. (The word translated "righteousness" in the A.V. is also capable of being translated "salvation"). It has ever been the Divine attitude. If His people turn to Him, He will turn to them. Those who sought Him would find the Divine blessing awaiting them. "It is time to seek Jehovah." If ever the words were applicable they are at the present day, in our perplexed and bewildered world of sin and apostasy. And the promise is still as applicable as it was centuries ago.

Hitherto Israel's behaviour had been diametrically opposed to what the prophet was now exhorting. He declared plainly that they had ploughed wickedness and reaped injustice. All standards had gone and, both in social life and in the religious sphere, they had engaged in wickedness. In the realm of morality they had practised evil. The only outcome was that they had suffered—and were still to suffer—the retributive injustice of enemies and oppressors. This had been their conduct. Reformation was overdue.

They had eaten the fruit of lies or of disappointment. They had played treacherously with God and with their rulers, but there was nothing satisfying in it. Their deceit had left them unsatisfied.

They had trusted in their chariots and warriors. The A.V. implies that their confidence had been in their own tortuous policies, but the significance seems rather that they had put their trust in the military forces, not of their own country but of Egypt and Assyria. These were utterly ineffectual and the prophet's call to repentance and to seeking after Jehovah might well have aroused the guilty people. But it was too late.

Therefore a tumult shall arise among your people, and all your fortresses shall be spoiled, as Shalman spoiled Beth-arbel on the day of battle. The mothers were dashed in pieces with their children. So shall it be done to you, O Bethel, because of your great wickedness: in the dawn shall the king of Israel be cut off (Hos. 10 : 14, 15).

The judgment was now unavoidable and the prophet heard the tumult or noise of the advancing Assyrian army. Before long the invaders would sweep over the land, destroying all the fortified cities and thereby removing the whole system of defence in which so much trust had been placed.

Hosea likened the destruction to that caused by Shalman at Beth-arbel in battle. Shalman was a Moabite tributary of Tiglath-pileser III, but the reference in verse 14 was probably to Shalmaneser IV (2 Kings 17 : 3). Beth-arbel seems to have been the Galilean town of Arbela (now Irbid). The incident referred to does not seem to be recorded elsewhere. The dashing of mothers to pieces with their children was not an uncommon occurrence with the brutal Assyrian soldiery.

As the centre of the calf-worship, Bethel had corrupted the country, and the idolatry and sinfulness of the people were regarded as centred there.. The judgment to fall upon Bethel was well merited. To crown the whole occurrence, the prophet declared that the king of Israel would be cut off at dawn. If the reference was to Hoshea, it was the end of the throne and of kingship for Israel. Divine judgment might take time, but it was inescapable.

130

CHAPTER 12

Base Ingratitude

THE principles of justice demanded the punishment of a guilty people for their transgressions: righteousness would otherwise have been a meaningless term. Yet heaven's love still reached out to them. The rebellious attitude seemed completely inexplicable in view of all that God had done for them, and His heart obviously ached at their appalling ingratitude.

GOD'S CALL

When Israel was a child, I loved him and called my son out of Egypt. The more they called them, the more they went from them. They sacrificed to the Baalim and burned incense to graven images (11 : 1, 2).

The Divine choice of Israel was an act of pure sovereignty and was not based upon the nation's merit or importance: it was the arbitrary demonstration of the love of the Eternal for an unworthy object. Jehovah's affection was set upon them from the earliest stage of their existence as a distinct nation, when they were utterly dependent upon Him. When Israel was nationally a child, Jehovah loved him, declared the prophet, and called His son out of Egypt.

He assumed the character and relationship of a Father in order to convey the wealth of His affection and compassion for one so undeserving. Israel was His son. The wonder of this amazing relationship should have thrilled the heart of the

131

nation. "The idea of the fatherhood of God," says McKeating (*op. cit.*, p. 137), "is neither peculiarly Christian nor peculiarly Biblical. The Baal-worshippers of Hosea's times were very familiar with the notion. Their high god, El, is father of the gods and is commonly entitled in the Canaanite texts, 'Father' of them." The concept was, therefore, doubly familiar to Israel, but it should none the less have aroused their devotion to Jehovah.

Because of His love for Israel, God called them out of the bondage of Egypt and delivered them from their oppressors and taskmasters. The deliverance from Egypt was repeatedly used by the prophets as the outstanding illustration of the exercise of God's power on behalf of His people. The salvation which they then experienced and the subsequent evidences of God's love, should have led them to humble service of Him, but instead they had rebelled against Him. It is interesting to note that Hosea's words regarding the call out of Egypt were taken up and applied to our Lord on the death of Herod (Matt. 2 : 15).

Prophets had been sent to win them back to the Divinely appointed way, but the more the prophets called them to repent and turn to God, the more determined were they to have their own way. The more they (the prophets) called, the more the nation turned away from the prophets and from Jehovah. (The R.S.V. renders "The more I called them, the more they went from me", which doubtless conveys the essential significance, but the Hebrew is clearly "they" and "them".)

Their apostasy was blatant. In place of Jehovah, they sacrificed to the Baalim and burnt incense to graven images. It was little wonder that judgment eventually fell. The service of Jehovah demanded holiness and purity and also denounced the use of any physical representation of Him (Exod. 19 : 6; 20 : 4). Yet they abandoned all this for the immorality and pollution of Baalism and for the idols considered to be symbols of the Deity. And all the time they were deaf to the warnings of the prophets who sought to bring them back to the ways of God.

DIVINE LOVE

I taught Ephraim also to walk, taking them by their arms; but they knew not that it was I who healed them. I drew them with cords of a man, with the bonds of love; and I was to them as the one who eases the yoke on their jaws and I gave food to them (11 : 3, 4).

Continuing the imagery of the paternal affection for the son, God declared that it was He who taught Ephraim to walk, holding him by the arms as he took his first tottering steps as a young child. All His tenderness and compassion were demonstrated in His care for the object of his mercy. It was He who helped the people to grow up into nationhood and preserved them from falling and bruising as they slowly advanced in experience and national awareness.

It was He who had healed them, yet they declined to recognise the fact. Apart from the obvious metaphorical sense, the healing was true in a literal sense, as in the case of the brazen serpent in the wilderness (Num. 21 : 8, 9). Indeed, one of Jehovah's titles was "Jehovah who heals you" (Exod. 15 : 26). How could they possibly ignore His goodness to them?

Even when Israel had developed and had grown to adulthood as a state and a people, Jehovah's solicitude was still demonstrated. Comparing Himself to the herdsman who drove the heifer which toiled for him, He said that He drew the animal by cords or rope, as a man would, but they were cords of love. At least one expositor interprets this particular symbolism as representing a man's wooing of a woman and his drawing out of her affections and ultimate allegiance by cords of love. But the remainder of the verse makes it clear that the imagery belongs to the fields.. No harsh driving was Jehovah's: in consideration for the people He eased the strain and burden and compassionately led them instead of driving them.

Still in the character of the considerate master, He said that He lifted the yoke from their jaws and liberated them for eating, and then set food before them. What the drover would do, who cared for his animals, so God had done for His people, Israel. The R.S.V. possibly makes this even clearer by its rendering, "I bent down to them and fed them," and George Adam Smith says, " and gently would I give them to eat." It seems incredible that they could ignore His mercy and compassion. Yet they are not isolated in this and the words still need to be conned over today.

THE ASSYRIAN FOE

He shall return to the land of Egypt, but the Assyrian shall be his king, because they refused to return. The sword shall whirl about his cities and shall consume his bars and devour them, because of their own counsels (Hos. 11 : 5, 6).

The A.V. states that he, i.e., Ephraim, shall not return to Egypt, but there is some support for the omission of the negative and this also conforms with Hos. 8 : 13. If the statement is regarded as a positive one, viz., that Israel would return to Egypt, the reference was presumably to the refugees who would flee to that country when Tiglath-pileser III swept over Israel. It was ironical that those, whose fathers had been Divinely delivered from Egypt, should seek refuge in the very land in which their ancestors had been oppressed. It was in direct disobedience to God's injunction that they should not return there any more (Deut. 17 : 16).

Because Israel had refused to turn to Jehovah, it was by His permissive will that Assyria had overrun the country, and it was not Egypt but Assyria which was to be recognised as the ruler of Israel. Their king, Hoshea, would be only a vassal of the Assyrians and the conquerers would make their rule felt. The people had rejected the guiding and educative hand of a Father God, had refused His love and compassion, and had declined to return to Him. They were now to pay the penalty for their folly.

134

Like the sword of Damocles, the sword of the Assyrians would hang over the people's heads. The prophet depicted it as whirling about over their cities, threatening the devastation which was still to come. Already the armies had carried out their ruthless activities, but worse was to come when Hoshea withheld the tribute payable to Assyria, and negotiated for assistance with So, king of Egypt (2 Kings 17 : 4), invoking—as might have been anticipated—a bitter retribution from Shalmaneser.

The prophet predicted the complete destruction of all Israel's defences. The bars of the gates would be destroyed so that no city would be able to withstand the invader, and the final blow would fall upon every city. Those, who so inadvisedly counselled king Hoshea to seek help from Egypt and to revolt against Assyria, would themselves be swept away. Their counsels were the cause of their country's fate. The conspiracy in which they had engaged would completely fail and they would pay the price for their treachery.

DELIBERATE BACKSLIDING

My people are bent on turning away from me. Though they called them upwards, none at all will lift himself up (Hos. 11 : 7).

In the eyes of Hosea, the people of Israel were deliberate backsliders, who were determined not to turn to Jehovah. Their bias was, in fact, to turn away from Him. They were God's elect people and no other could come to their aid, but they were imbued with the spirit of rebellion and seemed oblivious to the consequences.

When the prophet exhorted them to repent and to turn to Jehovah, to look upwards and to change the whole course of their lives, they declined to listen. As another says, "they could not be lifted from the rut of demoralisation in which they were sunk". In their moral apathy, they had no desire to lift themselves up.

Horton (*op. cit.*, p. 61) takes the view that those who called

135

on the people to amend their ways were not the prophets but the rulers. "Though the boastful king and his counsellors appeal to heaven," he writes, "and direct the people's thoughts to God, they will not lift up the degraded people; God has withdrawn; the religious talk is unreal." In conformity with verse 2, however, it seems more reasonable to regard the messengers as the prophets; it could scarcely be claimed that the king and the court in any way sought to lead the people heavenward.

THE LOVE OF GOD

How can I give you up, Ephraim? How can I surrender you, Israel? How can I make you like Admah? How can I set you like Zeboim? My heart is turned within me. My compassions are kindled together. I will not execute my fierce anger, I will not turn to destroy Ephraim. For I am God (El) and not man, the Holy One in your midst, and I will not come in wrath into the city (Hos. 11 : 8, 9).

The fate of a stubborn and rebellious son under the law was to be stoned to death (Deut. 21 : 18–21). Jehovah had clearly demonstrated the rebelliousness of His son, Israel. The despite done to His love, the flaunting of His mercy and compassion, and the deliberate revolt against His will, constituted an indictment to which there was no defence. The legal penalty must inevitably be exacted. Logic would have anticipated a plain declaration that, with the Assyrian invasion, the nation of Israel would be permanently exterminated, never again to be revived. But God's ways are not man's ways nor His thoughts man's thoughts.

When unmitigated punishment should have been meted out, the yearning love of God's heart asserted itself and broke out in irrepressible tenderness. Daringly the prophet portrayed the conflict between justice and mercy in the courts of heaven. In a series of rhetorical questions, Jehovah posed the problem of how His infinite love could deliver up His son to the well-merited punishment. "How can I give you up, Ephraim?

136

How can I surrender you, Israel?" It was just that the sword of judgment should fall upon the recalcitrant nation, but were all the Divine purposes thus to be frustrated? How could He surrender His beloved?

Admah and Zeboim, cities of the plain, were completely annihilated in the judgment on Sodom and Gomorrah (Deut. 29 : 22, 23). Was God to allow a similar fate for Israel? Punishment was certainly to be inflicted as the prophet had so explicitly predicted. Was it to involve the complete extirpation of God's people? The justification for it could not be questioned, but God does not delight in destruction.

He declared that His heart recoiled within Him and that His compassions were kindled: He "was wholly overcome with sympathy", as one translation renders it. He had chosen Israel as His son and had covenanted with him in grace. His purposes could not be thwarted nor His covenant revoked. Even if judgment fell, mercy must find a way of escape.

Consequently He declared that He would not execute His fierce anger. This was no concession to sin, and certainly no restriction of the punishment due. It was rather an intimation that, whatever Israel's experiences and whatever judgment fell upon them, He would not entirely obliterate them. The Divine relationship could not be terminated: it would continue for ever. He had trained and made a nation of Israel: it was not His purpose now to destroy that nation.

None could question His will, He is the mighty God and the Holy One in the midst of his people. He would purge out the dross that the remainder might be sanctified to Him. Then, emphatically, He affirmed, He would not come into the city (presumably Samaria) in wrath, which would have implied its complete and final destruction. Justice would be tempered with mercy.

THE LION'S CALL

They shall go after Jehovah. He shall roar like u lion. When he shall roar, then sons shall hasten from the west. They

137

shall hasten like birds out of Egypt and like doves out of the land of Assyria: and I will cause them to dwell in their homes, says Jehovah (Hos. 11 : 10, 11).

Punishment for sin was to be meted out and the exile to Assyria was a just recompense for Israel's transgressions. If the judgment was to be tempered with mercy and the total extermination of the people was not determined, then the Holy One of Israel must not only stay the hand of the oppressor but also undertake the nation's repatriation and rehabilitation. This the prophet logically predicted.

Hosea had previously depicted Jehovah as a lion (*shaehal*), ravaging and tearing His people (Hos. 5 : 14), but now he used the same metaphor in a totally different sense, even employing a different substantive, *aryeh,* to emphasise the difference. The people, he prophesied, would go after Jehovah, because He would roar like a lion, summoning the young lions to Himself. That mighty roar would summon His people from captivity to return to their own land.

The prophet clearly anticipated a day which is still future, since the events of which he spoke have not yet been fulfilled in history. The presence of Jehovah in all His power and might and the mighty lion's roar which was to issue forth at His coming, were presumably a picture of the Divine intervention in human affairs at the Second Advent of Christ. When the forces of the world's states are gathered together against the little country of Israel, and there is no helper to relieve the city of Jerusalem, the Messiah will come with all His forces to deliver His people (Zech. 14 : 4). It is at that time that He will summon the exiles to return (Ezek. 36 : 24).

At the sound of the lion's roar, Hosea foretold that the young lions (or "sons") would come hurrying from the west. They had fled to the west at the threat of the invader, but their descendants will hear the call to return because deliverance has come. The return of nearly three million Jews to Israel since the first world war—many inspired by fear of death in Central Europe—is perhaps a foreshadowing

138

of the great regathering from the west which has still to occur. The A.V. and R.S.V. suggest that they will come trembling and possibly humbled in spirit, but the emphasis seems rather upon their haste to return when they hear the summons.

While the majority of the people were deported to Assyria, many sought refuge in Egypt when their land was devastated by the invader. Hosea declared that they would return with haste like birds out of Egypt and doves out of the land of Assyria. The dove was proverbial for its swiftness of flight; it flew even faster when frightened, and the prophet portrayed the people trembling with eagerness as they hasten back to their own land. The simile of the dove was even more suitable because the dove always returns as soon as possible to its nest (Isa. 60 : 8).

When that day comes, God will bring back His people from every direction and restore them once more to their own land. He has pledged Himself to return them to their own houses and homes. He will cause them to dwell once more in the places from which their ancestors were forcibly removed. The prophets combine to testify that there is yet to be a future for Israel in the purposes of God.

EPHRAIM'S DECEIT

Ephraim encompasses me about with lies and the house of Israel with deceit. Judah is yet wayward towards God (El) and towards the Holy One who is faithful (Hos. 11 : 12).

In the Hebrew Bible, Hos. 11 : 12 was the first verse of chapter 12.

It seems extraordinary that, at the very moment when the pledge of restoration was being given, the prophet was compelled to allude to the deceitfulness of his people, which was so often a hindrance to Divine blessing. Their ancestor, Jacob, was known as a deceiver and had been a supplanter from the womb. His unfortunate characteristics had been preserved in his descendants.

Hosea portrayed Jehovah as surrounded by Ephraim's lies

and deceit, as though He was completely hedged in by the people's falsehoods. Their manoeuvrings with Egypt and Assyria and their tortuous political intrigues well merited the expressions used. But the implication was that Jehovah's purposes of blessing were being obstructed because of the unfaithfulness of His people.

Even Judah had ignored the warnings addressed to her sister kingdom and was oblivious to the lesson of God's judgment upon her. With all the additional privileges of the temple, its priesthood and offerings and the teaching throughout the land, Judah was wayward towards God, roving unrestrainedly like an animal that had broken loose. The Holy One had proved His faithfulness to her, but she showed no deference to Him or to His admonitions and warnings. It was a sad commentary on a land so favoured. But others more favoured in a later day have proved equally culpable.

CHAPTER 13

Jacob's Provocation

DESPITE the manifested compassion of God and the expression of His intention to restore His people to their own land and to settle them once more in security, Israel's behaviour was unchanged. Hosea 11 closed with the picture of Ephraim surrounding Jehovah with a hedge of falsehood and deception, and the next chapter opened with the nation increasing its offence and indulging still more in lies, fraud and violence. It is almost incomprehensible that a people should be so blind to the significance of their conduct.

AN EMPTY POLICY

Ephraim feeds on wind and pursues the east wind. Daily he increases lies and violence; and they make a covenant with Assyria, and carry oil to Egypt (Hos. 12 : 1).

In remarkable imagery the prophet depicted the senseless folly in which Israel indulged. He described Ephraim as feeding upon wind and pursuing the east wind—pointless and impossible occupations. The wind was empty and elusive and could provide no food for even the most hungry. If the R.S.V. "herds the wind" is adopted, there was no more value in the action, for the wind was uncontrollable and beyond subjection to human will.

The east wind, to which the prophet referred, was the sirocco, the dry withering blast from the desert, which seared and scorched the vegetation and menaced man and beast. No one would seek the sirocco, yet Hosea described Israel as pursuing it. By inference, the political policies of the nation were equally foolish: they were tantamount to seeking the empty and unsatisfying and hunting after that which only brought heat, discomfort and destruction.

At the same time, Israel continuously increased its falsehood and violence. As the next sentence made clear, the prophet was referring to the disastrous changes of policy of king Hoshea. He made a treaty with Assyria, but then turned to Egypt for help in breaking it (2 Kings 17 : 3, 4), thereby bringing upon himself and his country the blast of the hot sirocco—the anger of Assyria. In the words of the prophet, they made a treaty with Assyria but, simultaneously, carried oil to Egypt.

Oil was a staple product of the country and was an apt figure for the wealth which Hoshea sent to Egypt to secure the help of that country (Isa. 30 : 6, 7). The deceit displayed in the king's dealings with Assyria reacted upon him in the desolation inflicted by Assyria upon him and his land. He proved conclusively that duplicity never pays, as Hosea clearly implied.

INDICTMENT OF JACOB

Jehovah has a controversy with Judah and will punish Jacob according to his ways; according to his deeds will he requite him (Hos. 12 : 2).

As previously (e.g., Hos. 4 : 1), the prophet set his words in the context of a legal court, with Jehovah as the plaintiff and the nation as the defendant. The case against the people was made against Jacob as their representative. Most versions indicate that the legal suit was against Judah. The introduction of the southern kingdom at this particular point seems inappropriate and it is usually considered that the word should be read as "Jacob". It is true that Judah at this time was following the evil example of Israel, but the latter part of the

142

chapter is concerned with Ephraim or Israel, with Jacob as their representative.

The character and deeds of their ancestor Jacob were being reproduced in his descendants. His dissimulation and deceitfulness had become their inalienable heritage, and the whole legal case presented by Jehovah was on the basis of Jacob's career. Heredity is not a fact which can be ignored and the principal characteristics of the parent are usually reproduced in the children. Only the grace and power of God can effect any change. But Israel bore the image of their ancestor firmly impressed upon their nature and character.

This did not excuse their conduct or relieve them of responsibility for their actions, and Jehovah declared that He would punish Jacob fittingly for his ways and requite him for his deeds. In perfect equity, the judgment would be suited to what had been done.

THE SUPPLANTER

In the womb he took his brother by the heel, and in his strength he had power as a prince with God. He had power over the angel and prevailed. He wept and made supplication to him. He found him in Bethel and there he spoke with us; even Jehovah Elohim of hosts; Jehovah is his memorial (Hos. 12 : 3–5).

The exposure of Jacob's trickery went back to his prenatal experience. His brother Esau was born first, but Jacob's hand seized his brother's heel, as though seeking already to supplant him (Gen. 25 : 26). The Hebrew *hahkab* (took by the heel) was the root of the name Jacob, by which he was called: later, he received the name Israel, derived from the root *sahrab* (had power as a prince). He certainly supplanted his brother by deceit and received the blessing of the firstborn instead of Esau (Gen. 27 : 36).

If the prophet recorded this shameful episode, he also quoted the more attractive incident at Peniel when, as a fullgrown man, Jacob wrestled with an unknown all night until

143

daybreak, suffering the putting out of joint of his thigh. There, according to the Scriptural account, he wrestled with God and was renamed Israel (Gen. 32 : 28).

Hosea revealed what had not been previously disclosed in the Genesis record, viz., that Jacob wept in his supplication to the One with whom he had wrestled all night. The prophet also referred to his wrestling with "the angel", indicating clearly that it was with the "angel of Jehovah" or the "angel of the covenant". The theophanic appearance at Peniel was of the Second Person of the Holy Trinity, to whom this title always belonged.

The prophet referred to the third episode in the patriarch's life when he met Jehovah at Bethel (Gen. 35 : 9–15). He had previously had a vision of Jehovah at the same place years earlier when he fled from home (Gen. 28 : 10–22), but it was evidently to the later occasion that Hosea alluded. God spoke to Israel's forefather there, but the prophet stated that "He spoke with us", envisioning the nation as personified in Jacob and emphasising the relationship with God. It was at Bethel that Jehovah confirmed the name of Israel and promised that the patriarch should be the founder of a nation, the father of other nations and the ancestor of kings, and once more pledging that the territory promised to Abraham and Isaac should be the property of Jacob and his descendants. By implication, these promises were made to the nation of Israel, since God was deemed to have spoken to them and not merely to Jacob.

The One who spoke to Jacob was no other than Jehovah Elohim of hosts, the Almighty God whose self-existence was virtually expressed by His name Jehovah. According to Horton (*op. cit.,* p. 64), "On the great Day of Atonement, the high priest pronounced the name ten times, and all the people fell on their faces, saying, 'Blessed be the glorious name of His kingdom for ever and ever.' . . . After 322 B.C., the time of Simon the Just, the high priest disused it for fear that its sanctity should be violated." This was the name by which God made Himself known to Israel, so that they might realise

His eternal and self-existent being and thereby be freed from any possible entanglement with false deities who were lifeless and impotent.

THE EFFECT

Therefore, return to your God (Elohim). Keep loving kindness and justice, and wait on your God (Elohim) continually (Hos. 12 : 6).

In view of the reminder of the greatness of God and the favour He had shown them in the person of their ancestor, there was no need for Israel to be concerned about their destiny or their welfare. There was assuredly no necessity for the people to attempt to determine their own future or to plan the best way of achieving it. Rather should they return to their God in meekness and humility.

Returning to God involved more than a mere nominal act: it implied a complete change of life—the jettisoning of the deceit and dissimulation which had characterised them, the repentance for the injustice to neighbour and nation, and the acknowledgment of the duties due to God and man. They should hold fast to lovingkindness and justice, demonstrating the genuineness of their turning to God by a new integrity and uprightness.

Moreover, instead of scheming and intriguing on their own behalf and demonstrating thereby their confidence in their own ability, they should show their confidence in God by waiting continually upon Him and allowing Him to act in the lives of themselves and in the nation as He pleased. This is precisely where men so often fail. It is so difficult to remain quiescent, leaving God to operate in life, instead of making one's own decisions and judging the appropriate action to take in self-protection or for self-advancement. But there is no other way for the one who submits to the Divine will and surrenders his life to God.

Canaan, false balances are in his hand; he loves to defraud. Ephraim said, Surely I have become rich. I have gained wealth for myself; all my profits shall bring me no iniquity that was a sin (Hos. 12 : 7, 8).

The Canaanites, whom Israel had dispossessed of their land, were a nation of traders, inhabiting the Phoenician coastal area, and the name Canaan or Canaanite in time became a synonym for merchant (Job 41 : 6; Prov. 31 : 24; Ezek. 17 : 4; Zeph. 1 : 11). Unfortunately, their reputation for honesty was extremely low; they were unscrupulous and were not averse to fraudulent commercial transactions.

Israel had settled down in Canaan and had assimilated the characteristics and outlook of their pagan neighbours. They adopted the same dishonest practices and crookedness, and were scarcely distinguishable from the Canaanites. In scorching tones of reproach, Jehovah addressed them in one word, "Canaan", a pejorative indicative of the degenerate state of His people.

He detected the false balances in their hands, a practice prohibited by the law (Lev. 19 : 35, 36; Deut. 25 : 13) and which the Scriptures described as an "abomination to Jehovah" (Prov. 11 : 1). It was not an uncommon practice for merchants to use different weights for buying and selling and deliberately to cheat their customers. The people of Israel, as other prophets make clear, had adopted the same fraudulent procedure. Their object was to make money by any means, and the prophet said that they loved to defraud.

Homer said that the Canaanites or Phoenicians were infamous for their greed and that they were commonly known as money-lovers. The opprobrium which attached to them now attached to Israel as well. They were as much dishonest traffickers as the Canaanites whom they had originally been commanded to destroy.

As though material possessions were the only thing which mattered, Ephraim boasted that they had become rich and

146

had gained wealth for themselves. But while congratulating themselves on their gains, they ignored the fact that their wealth had not always been legitimately acquired. In fact, they claimed that none of the profits they had made had been the cause of their committing any iniquity serious enough to be described as sin. In their insensate folly, they deemed any departure from the path of strict rectitude as a trifling lapse which could, in no circumstances, be reckoned as sin. Fraud, dishonesty and oppression were of no account.

That people, who knew the infinite holiness and strict righteousness of God, should consider any deviation from the path of absolute honesty as a triviality seems almost incomprehensible. Yet there was little to distinguish them from some who profess today to be followers of Christ. Business morality is not always of the highest order, and not infrequently actions are taken which a more scrupulous conscience might regard as questionable. But this kind of conduct is deemed as relatively unimportant or else as essential, and those who indulge in it regard themselves as irreproachable. The omniscient Lord is not ignorant of the ways of His followers and His standards have not been lowered.

DIVINE DISCIPLINE

And I, Jehovah your Elohim from the land of Egypt, will again make you dwell in tents, as in the days of the appointed feast. I spoke to the prophets and I multiplied visions and used parables by the hand of the prophets (Hos. 12 : 9, 10).

Israel's Canaanised mode of existence was nothing but unrelieved worldliness. It conformed to the ways of the pagan world around them and was a virtual denial of the uncompromising holiness of God. Yet Jehovah was the God they had known from the land of Egypt; by implication He was the One who had delivered and protected them and ultimately settled them in a land for which they had not laboured.

He could not allow the nation to continue its course unchecked. He indicated that the people would be driven out of their comfortable homes and luxurious dwellings, their profitable trading and cultivated fields, to live again the nomadic tent life they had known in the wilderness.

During the Feast of Tabernacles, they constructed booths in which to live for the whole week (Lev. 23 : 42), and God used this figure to symbolise the experience through which they were to pass. The tent life in the wilderness prepared them by its trials and tribulations for their future enjoyment of the promised land. The feast, which took place at the gathering of the harvest and was a time of rejoicing, was a reminder of the goodness of God in the things of nature. The experience threatened by Jehovah was, therefore, with the object of teaching them again their complete dependence upon Him and the emptiness and inconsistency of their own ways.

He reminded them that they had never been without Divine warnings. If calamity came upon them for their evil ways, they could never plead that God's way had not been made clear. He had spoken to the prophets who had conveyed His word to the people. He had used visions and parables to make the message clear to the prophets and through them to the people. It was all the more deplorable, therefore, that they should have pursued a course so entirely contrary to His will and have thereby invoked inevitable punishment.

GILEAD AND GILGAL

If there is iniquity in Gilead, they shall surely become vanity. They sacrifice bullocks in Gilgal, so their altars shall be like stone heaps in the fields (Hos. 12 : 11).

The prophet had already denounced the town of Gilead on the east of Jordan for its iniquity and murder (Hos. 6 : 8, 9) and he now declared that if iniquity was to be found there— as it was commonly known to be— the inhabitants would become nothing. Gilead was wholly given up to idolatry and the prophet's words of reprobation were justified. What he implicitly predicted as their fate actually came to pass (2 Kings 15 : 29).

148

Gilgal, on the west of Jordan, was equally culpable. The altars erected at the idolatrous shrine were dedicated, some to the calf-worship and some to Baalism, and the site was, therefore, doubly guilty. There they sacrificed bullocks in an affront to the true God. In consequence, Hosea warned that their altars would become like the heaped stones which the farmer piled up in the ploughed fields, and of no more value to the worshippers than such heaps (*gallim*, heaps, was a play on the word Gilgal). Ehrlich suggests that "heaps" should be rendered as "dung-droppings", implying that the altars were as numerous and objectionable as the droppings of animals found in the furrows of the fields they had ploughed, but this is a little far-fetched.

EARLY EXPERIENCES

Jacob fled to the land of Aram, and Israel served for a wife, and for a wife he tended sheep. By a prophet Jehovah brought up Israel out of Egypt, and by a prophet was he preserved (Hos. 12 : 12, 13).

Turning from the commercial malpractices and the sinful idolatry of the people, which were to invoke the Divine punishment, Hosea reverted once more to the didactic history of Jacob as illustrative of God's dealings with Israel.

Because of Esau's anger against his brother, Isaac sent Jacob away from home to his brother-in-law, Laban, of Padanaram (Gen. 28 : 5). For love of a wife Jacob (or Israel, as he subsequently became) served his uncle by tending sheep and cattle (Gen. 29 : 18–20; 31 : 38–41), work which was considered one of the hardest forms of service. The manner in which Jehovah had watched over their ancestor should have been an illustration to the nation of the Divine care and consideration for them.

At the same time, it was a reminder of their ancestor's unworthiness (and consequently of theirs also) of the grace of God. As Calvin says, "Their father Jacob, who was he? What was his condition? . . . He was a fugitive from his country.

Even if he had always lived at home, his father was only a stranger in the land. But he was compelled to flee into Syria. And how splendidly did he live there? He was with his uncle, no doubt, but he was treated quite meanly as any common slave; he served for a wife. And how did he serve? He was the man who tended the cattle."

Jacob's descendants were slaves in Egypt, but by a prophet, Hosea recalled, Jehovah brought up Israel out of Egypt and by a prophet were they preserved. The reference, of course, was to Moses, aptly described in Deut. 34 : 10 as a prophet. It was under the leadership of Moses that the people were delivered from the bondage of Egypt and brought safely through the wilderness. How could they despise the ways of God when His care for the nation had been so great and had been exercised so consistently? There may also have been the implication that, even if justice demanded the punishment just announced, Jehovah's compassion would still be shown and He would not leave them in exile and tribulation.

PROVOCATION

Ephraim provoked him to anger most bitterly. Therefore shall he leave his blood upon him, and his reproach shall his Lord (Adonai) turn back upon him (Hos. 12 : 14).

Despite all the mercy and compassion displayed by Jehovah, the nation had bitterly provoked Him. To their commercial dishonesty and their defiling idolatry (vv. 7 and 11), was added a further cause of provocation in their blood-guiltiness. Details were not specified of the practices or incidents concerned, but it is possible that the prophet was alluding, *inter alia,* to the sacrificing of children in the fire to the god Moloch (2 Kings 17 : 17, 18). This was an intolerable abomination to Jehovah.

The nation's culpability was evident and could not be ignored. The provocation demanded retribution and God declared that Israel must bear the consequences of his wrongdoing. Their blood-guiltiness would be left upon them, with the plain and unavoidable invocation to judgment. Moreover, their reproach—the insult offered to God by the idolatrous rites of Baalism—would recoil upon the people's heads. Ephraim's character and conduct were such that the Almighty could not ignore them, and justice demanded punishment.

CHAPTER 14

Continuance in Sin

THROUGHOUT Hosea's ministry the nation's service to Baal was repeatedly exposed as sinful idolatry and tacitly as an insult to Jehovah. The prophet also inveighed against the sin because of its effect upon the conduct and morality of the people. Here was something so defiling that it contaminated all who touched it. But Israel seemed bent on observing the Canaanite cult and rejecting God. His exhortations and warnings seemed ineffectual in achieving any change in the polluted people, and He intimated even more clearly the inevitable result of their attitude.

IDOLS OF BAAL

When Ephraim spoke there was trembling. He exalted himself in Israel. But when he transgressed through Baal, he died. And now they add to their sin more and more, and make for themselves molten images of their silver and idols according to their own skill, all of it the work of the craftsman. To them do they speak. Let the men who sacrifice kiss the calves (Hos. 13 : 1, 2).

When, on his deathbed, Jacob blessed the heads of the twelve tribes of Israel, he gave Ephraim a special place of blessing in Israel (Gen. 48 : 14–20) and that tribe seems to have taken a place of superiority among the tribes. When Ephraim spoke, others trembled, and the tribe was recognised as important among the ten tribes. Cheyne takes a slightly different line when he says (*op. cit.*, p. 119), "When the Ephraimites in trembling accents responded to the divine call . . . , they rose to the exalted position which its prophetic ancestor foreshadowed (Gen. 49 : 22–26). The reference is partly to the leadership of the Ephraimite Joshua, partly to the prosperity which attended the tribe of Ephraim even when it no longer supplied a general or judge or a king to the entire nation."

What was true of Ephraim was true of the nation as a whole. They might have been used of God as His witness to the world. When they were in communion with Him and walked humbly before Him, Israel were exalted. But when they transgressed through Baal (1 Kings 16 : 31), the nation virtually died. The lapse into Baalism signed the nation's death warrant. The execution of the sentence did not occur immediately, but the destructive work had already begun. The ten tribes severed themselves from the worship and teaching of Jehovah when they deliberately corrupted their religion and taught that Baal had superseded Jehovah as their benefactor in the gifts of nature.

They increasingly added to their sin, said the prophet, by making molten images of silver and idols skilfully constructed by craftsmen. These were their gods. It has been suggested that the idols were figurines of the golden calves, constructed for use primarily in private worship, but it seems more probable that they were images of Baal and Ashtoreth. They had known the true God and had substituted graven images for Him, declaring that the prosperity of the fields was due to the nature gods rather than to Jehovah Their spiritual life had died. There could be no communion with Jehovah by idol-worshippers who gave themselves to the polluting rites of nature worship. To these deaf and dumb idols people addressed their words of homage and petition. Nothing could be more patently absurd than to supplicate their own handiwork for help and blessing.

The last sentence of verse 2 presents difficulties in interpretation. One version renders the words, "Let sacrificers of men kiss the calves," but it is improbable that human sacrifices (other than to Moloch) had been indulged in, and the rendering above probably gives the correct sense. Kissing was an act of homage (1 Kings 19 : 18), and the worshippers of the golden calves apparently paid their respect to the idols in this fashion. And these were men who had known Jehovah. Herein lay the seriousness of their conduct.

NO FUTURE

Therefore they shall be like the morning mist, and like the dew which early passes away, like the chaff which is driven by the whirlwind out of the threshing floor and like smoke out of the chimney (Hos. 13 : 3).

Hosea devastatingly implied that there was no future for Israel. Their sins constantly increased and there was no respect for God. Therefore, he declared, they would be like the evanescent morning mist or like the early dew, which disappeared as soon as the rays of the sun made their presence felt. They would be just as impermanent as the dissolving mist.

Their future was as uncertain as the chaff whirled out of the threshing-floor by a tempestuous whirlwind—presumably a reminder of the violence and suddenness with which they would be swept out of the land. They were no more permanent than the smoke which escaped through the hole in the roof. Security and stability were no longer theirs.

Whether they realised the significance of the prophet's words or not, the implication was perfectly clear. Judgment had been pronounced upon the nation: it was to take the form of complete removal from the land by the Assyrians, and this was to happen suddenly and their deportation would be a swift operation. They should have understood and the intimation should have stirred them to true repentance, but it seemed to have no effect whatsoever.

I am Jehovah your Elohim from the land of Egypt, and you shall know no God (Elohim) but me: for there is no saviour besides me. I knew you in the wilderness in the land of drought. According to their pasture they were filled. They were filled and their heart was lifted up; therefore they forgot me (Hos. 13 : 4–6).

The first clause of verse 4 repeated the first clause of Hos. 12 : 9 (cf. Exod. 20 : 1). Jehovah was the God whom the people had known from Egypt: by implication, He was the source of their deliverance and blessing. "You shall have no other gods before me," ran the first command of the decalogue (Exod. 20 : 3), and the words were reiterated in the ears of this later generation. "There is no saviour besides me," declared Jehovah (Isa. 43 : 11). No other deity had been responsible for their deliverance from Egypt, their preservation through the wilderness or their possession of the promised land. Jehovah alone demanded their homage and allegiance. They were indebted solely to Jehovah. Their experience confirmed that their help had been in Him and in no other. Justifiably He expostulated with Israel for her rejection of Him.

It was Jehovah who had known Israel in the wilderness, in the land of drought (Deut. 8 : 15). Throughout the barren wilderness, where there was neither food nor water, He had provided for their needs and had shielded them from dangers and foes. Their history was one of the saving grace of God. How could they but acknowledge Him as the source of their every blessing?

Yet, said the prophet, the more pasture they had, the more they ate themselves to the full, and when their hunger was satisfied their heart was lifted up and they forgot Jehovah, the source of all these good gifts. It was from this that their ultimate apostasy sprang. They enjoyed the gifts of God's hand without a thought of Him and without an expression of gratitude to Him. They focused their attention only upon their satisfaction and lost sight of their great Benefactor.

Even worse, their heart was lifted up in pride and self-exaltation and finally the spirit of rebellion prevailed and they turned against Him. It has ever been thus. In 1948, 1956 and 1967 the present State of Israel recognised that victory had been won for them, not by their own strength or military might, but by the intervention of Almighty God. But very quickly they forgot and were soon attributing their salvation to their own effort and strategy and military leadership. Nor can the Christian claim to be different in character. How often we seek God's help and blessing, only to forget Him when the answer comes!

THE DIVINE ANSWER

Therefore, I will be to them like a lion; like the leopard will I lurk beside the way. I will fall upon them like a bear robbed of its young, and will tear the caul of their heart, and there will I devour them like a lioness: the wild beast shall rend them (Hos. 13 : 7, 8).

Throughout Israel's history, Jehovah had been their shepherd and protector, but now, in startling theriomorphisms, He indicated the character of the wrath to be poured out upon them. He took up example after example of marauding beast in illustration of the curse they had invoked. The terrifying imagery indicated the extent of the unmitigated punishment to be meted out.

He would become to them like a lion in all its fierceness. None could deliver from the king of beasts seeking its prey. There was no intimation of mercy now: unhestitatingly and irresistibly the lion would come upon its prey and carry it away to its lair.

The destroyer would assume the character of the leopard with all its swiftness. The leopard usually sprang upon the unwary animal from an ambush. So, said Jehovah, He would lurk in hiding beside the way, to pounce upon an unsuspecting Israel, and because of the swiftness of the attack, escape would be impossible.

156

He would meet them, He declared, like a she-bear robbed of her cubs. All the savage ferocity and fury of the bear would be raised to the extreme by the loss of her young, and nothing could withstand her awful onslaught. As a bear, He would rend the caul of their heart, or tear open their breast. Their hardened hearts, which had been impervious to the pleas to repentance, would now metaphorically be torn open in fury. The bear would strike directly at the heart of its prey.

Like a lioness He would devour them, not in a sudden attack, but quietly consuming the prey in the peace and quiet of the lions' den.

Again He declared that the wild beast would rend them, as though calling upon every other wild animal of the jungle to complete the destruction.

Only too certainly were the threats implemented. The Assyrians ravaged the country in 734 B.C. Nine years later they invested the city of Samaria and by 721 B.C. the whole of the population had been carried into captivity. The judgment of God was complete. The history is a fearful reminder of the wrath of the Almighty upon those who do despite to Him.

THE ONLY HELP

O Israel, you have destroyed yourself; but in me is your help (Hos. 13 : 9).

The R.S.V. renders verse 9, "I will destroy you, O Israel; who can help you?" This, however, seems to be without very much support. Horton's wording, although free seems more appropriate: "This is your destruction, O Israel, that to me, your helper, you have been unfaithful." A Jewish commentator's rendering is, "O Israel, by revolting against me, who am ready to help you at all times, you have destroyed yourself." The implication of the verse is that the nation's ruin was brought about by herself.

By their folly and their apostasy, the nation had invoked God's judgment upon them. While Jehovah had used instru-

ments to effect His purpose and had wrought their destruction
by these instruments, it was Israel's own failure which had
really caused the Divine action. If destruction had come upon
them by the hand of God, in consequence of their own
actions, whence could they look for help? Their only helper
was Jehovah, but they had alienated His sympathy and mercy.
There was no other direction in which they could look for
help. No other could come to their aid. Their position was,
therefore, utterly hopeless. Yet there was an implicit pledge
in the declaration that in Jehovah was their help. If they had
invoked judgment now, was there not a tacit implication that
they would not be utterly destroyed, but that a trust in
Jehovah would bring salvation at the appointed time?

THE KING

*Where is now your king that he may save you in all your
cities? And your judges of whom you said, Give me a king
and princes? I gave you kings in my anger and took them
away in my wrath (Hos. 13 : 10, 11).*

Israel had clamoured for a king that they might be like the
nations around them and that they might have someone to
judge them and fight their battles, and Jehovah had eventually
acceded to their request (1 Sam. 8 : 6–22). The prophet,
therefore, justifiably, albeit scornfully, addressed the question
to them, "Where is now your king that he may save you in all
your cities?" In the palace revolutions and repeated assassina-
tions, king had followed king, but there was no outstanding
leader. If Hoshea was on the throne at the time of Hosea's taunt-
ing enquiry, his ineptitude and indecisiveness did not evoke
any confidence. If he was already a captive of Shalmaneser V
(2 Kings 17 : 4), the situation was even more hopeless.

They had turned their backs on Jehovah and had continued
to place their reliance in their kings and princes (who shared
the judicial functions and were, therefore, referred to as
judges) who had so miserably failed them. Not one of the

158

usurpers who seized the throne was deserving of their trust in the critical juncture which now faced them.

Even after the partition of the kingdom, kings were still raised up to govern each nation. God declared that he gave them kings in His anger and took them away in His wrath. It was a historical fact. The procession of rulers who succeeded each other on a tottering throne was one which reflected no credit on throne or nation. They were given and taken away in punishment of the people, and their own worthless character reflected the Divine attitude to the institution and to His rebellious people. It has often been said that a nation gets the rulers it deserves (words which probably still have an application today) and it was certainly true in Israel's experience.

A DESPERATE SITUATION

The iniquity of Ephraim is bound up; his sin is laid by in store. The throes of a travailing woman shall come upon him: he is an unwise son; for he should not tarry in the place of the breaking forth of children (Hos. 13 : 12, 13).

God had made it clear that the destruction He had threatened was inescapable and that, with the constant change of rulers, there was no delivery for the guilty people. The full penalty for their wrongdoing was to be exacted. In picturesque language the prophet stated that Ephraim's iniquity was bound up and his sin laid by in store.

The allusion was to the practice of maintaining records of important events (Ezra 4 : 14–19). The documents were tied together and then stored in a depository for safe keeping (Deut. 32 : 34; Isa. 8 : 16). Hosea was warning Israel that the nation's misdeeds were being registered in the heavenly records: details of the accumulating transgressions were retained in the celestial archives. It might seem that punishment had been delayed or that no note had been taken of what was happening, but one day the records would be brought forth in evidence against the guilty. There was no escape from the fate towards which the nation was so rapidly being carried.

The New Testament makes it clear that an imperishable record is kept of the deeds of all mankind and that, at the final assize, sentence will be passed on the basis of the unerring records maintained in heaven (Rev. 20 : 12). It is a shattering thought that there is no escape for man from his actions: a day of reckoning is inevitable. Even for the Christian, it is patent that accountability cannot be avoided. His reward at the judgment seat of Christ will be based on what has been done in life (2 Cor. 5 : 10). A record is kept, the details of which cannot be disputed.

Hosea proceeded to describe the desperate circumstances in which the nation was found, and the imagery employed was remarkable. Hezekiah's message to Isaiah, following the threats uttered by Rabshakeh, compared the helpless situation of Judah in that day of trouble to the inability of a travailing woman to bring forth the child to be born (Isa. 37 : 3; 2 Kings 19 : 3). Hosea chose the same symbolism but placed the responsibility for failure upon the child and not the mother. In addition, he depicted Israel as both mother and child.

The agony and suffering to be experienced by Israel were so intense that he likened them to the labour pains of a travailing woman. The nation would no more be able to extricate themselves from the tribulation coming upon them than the woman could escape from her throes. Although the prophet's primary reference was to the trials and troubles to be experienced in the Assyrian invasion, the prediction unquestionably also anticipated the more terrible sufferings of the great tribulation during the day of Jehovah (Isa. 13 : 8). The immediate sufferings were, of course, the direct result of the iniquity and sin referred to in the preceding verse.

But Hosea compared the people with the unborn child as well as to the mother and described Israel as an unwise son. At the moment when birth was due, it was retarded because of the unwisdom of the child. In the natural realm, the life of mother and child would be endangered by such a retarding, and there may have been a tacit reference to this in the prophecy. Responsibility was attributed to the child. The wise child in the prophet's view, would be eager to leave the womb and to preserve the lives of himself and his mother thereby. Ephraim, with a supreme lack of judgment, was delaying his birth.

The dealings of God with Israel were intended to bring about the nation's repentance and metaphorical re-birth. As Mays (*op. cit.*, p. 180) says, Jehovah's "chastisement was the crucible of renewal, the painful preparation for a new covenant and a revived people." But Ephraim did not recognise the time and resisted a new birth. Well did the prophet describe him as an unwise son.

SALVATION

Shall I ransom them from the hand of Sheol? Shall I redeem them from death? Where are your plagues, O death? Where is your destruction, O Sheol? Compassion is hid from my eyes (Hos. 13 : 14).

The irreversibility of the Divine sentence upon Israel was made clear. They were faced with an implacable doom.

Although death and Sheol were used in the Old Testament as almost synonymous terms for the nether world (Psa. 6 : 5; 49 : 14; Isa. 28 : 15), the former was apparently employed of the state of those whose life had gone, while the latter usually implied the location of the dead. The record of Ephraim's guilt (verse 12) made it impossible, in the absence of any sign of repentance, for God's compassion to be demonstrated. He posed the rhetorical questions whether He should ransom them from the hand of Sheol or redeem them from death, but the questions required no answer. A ransom required the payment of a price to free a person from legal obligation. Redemption was the act of a kinsman on behalf of a relative. Neither was considered practicable in the case of unrepentant Ephraim.

Jehovah called for the plagues, or sicknesses, of death and

for the destruction of Sheol. Nothing was to withstand the activities of these alien powers (Psa. 9 : 6, 13). Israel must suffer the full penalty for their wrongdoing. They had rejected the opportunity of repentance and nothing could avert the impending judgment. Jehovah, who had shown such compassion in the past history of His people, now declared that compassion was hid from His eyes. In a future day that compassion will again be demonstrated but, at this juncture, punishment must be inflicted.

In his wonderful exposition of the Christian's hope, including the resurrection of the Christian dead, the apostle Paul quoted Hosea's words, imparting to the questions a new significance, however. "O death, where is your sting? O Hades (the Greek equivalent of Sheol), where is your victory?" he cried (1 Cor. 15 : 55). The "plagues" and "destruction" of Hosea gave place to the "sting" and "victory" of the apostle. For the child of God, death will then have no further hold and Hades no other victory. Both will be impotent before the power of the coming Christ.

DIVINE DESTRUCTION

Though he bear fruit among his brethren, an east wind shall come, the wind of Jehovah coming up from the desert, and his spring shall become dry, and his fountain shall be dried up. He shall spoil the treasure of all precious vessels (Hos. 13 : 15).

The certainty of the punishment was again asserted with different symbolism. Ephraim's name meant "fruitfulness" and Hosea pictured the nation bearing fruit among other nations, only to suffer complete and unexpected desolation. The R.S.V. renders the first clause, "Though he may flourish as the reed plant," and Mays interprets the clause as painting Ephraim flourishing as a plant among the reeds, but the authority for this is not clear.

The east wind, or sirocco, described as "the wind of Jehovah coming up from the desert", swept across the fruitful field and dried up the reservoirs and springs and destroyed the produce of the field. It was an apt symbol of the Assyrian invader devastating the country and laying it completely waste, in response to Jehovah's call for the plagues and destruction of death and Sheol.

In the last clause the disguise disappeared and the conqueror was plainly indicated. The ruthless Assyrian soldiers were to carry off to their own country all treasures of Israel—gold, silver and jewels—as, in fact, actually occurred. The judgment was to be complete.

THE METROPOLIS

Samaria shall bear her guilt, because she has rebelled against her God (Elohim). They shall fall by the sword; their children shall be dashed to pieces, and their women with child shall be ripped up (Hos. 13 : 16).

In the Hebrew Bible Hos. 13 : 16 is the first verse of the following chapter, but it is a not inappropriate conclusion to Hos. 13.

Samaria was the capital of the northern kingdom and the centre of the intrigues and revolutions and fundamentally of the rebellion against Jehovah. It was responsible for the apostasy against God and for the introduction of the worship of the golden calves and was ultimately responsible also for the national turning to Baalism and the immoral fertility cult. Samaria, therefore, must bear her guilt. Her crimes were firmly attached to her, and the basic one was plainly stated as her rebellion against God.

For this the merciless foe would exact the full penalty. The inhabitants would fall by the sword. The enemy would sweep into the city and butcher everyone in cold blood. The young children who played in the streets would, in sheer barbarity, be dashed to pieces. And the pregnant women would be ripped open—a fate only too common in warfare of the day and ensuring that no progeny were left to repopulate the city.

History records how completely Hosea's prediction was fulfilled.

Writing of the Assyrian methods in war, A. H. Sayce (*Assyria: Its Princes, Priests and People*, p. 127) says, "The barbarities which followed the capture of a town would be almost incredible, were they not a subject of boast in the inscriptions which record them. Assurnatsir-pal's cruelties were especially revolting. Pyramids of human heads marked the path of the conqueror; boys and girls were burnt alive or reserved for a worse fate; men were impaled, flayed alive, blinded, or deprived of their hands and feet, of their ears and noses, while the women and children were carried into slavery, the captured city plundered and reduced to ashes, and the trees in its neighbourhood cut down . . . How deeply seated was the thirst for blood and vengeance on an enemy is exemplified in a bas-relief which represents Assurbanipal and his queen feasting in their garden while the head of the conquered Elamite king hangs from a tree above."

Horton (*op. cit.*, p. 72), referring to the complete desolation of Samaria, writes, "Repeopled by heathen (2 Kings 17 : 24), destroyed by John Hyrcanus (Jos. *Ant.* xiii : 10, 3), fortified by Herod (Jos. *Ant.* xiv, 4, 4; 5, 3) and called Sebaste, after Augustus (Sebastos), showing on a coin of Nero found on the site the image, it is thought, of the old Ashtoreth, the traditional burying-place of John Baptist, rifled by Julian, then the see of a Christian bishopric, now known as Sebastieh, it offers no trace for ever of the powerful throne which once flourished there, and of the guilty people who there filled up the measure of their iniquities." The proud metropolis of Israel is today relatively unimportant.

CHAPTER 15

Return to Blessing

THE purposes of God can never be frustrated, either by the active opposition of the enemy or by the failure of His people. Jehovah entered into an irrevocable covenant with Abraham which must be implemented in the ultimate blessing of Israel. Nothing can thwart His intention and His pledges can neither be annulled nor abrogated. Eventually, therefore, a guilty Israel must be brought to repentance and to an acknowledgment of Jehovah as the One against whom she has sinned, and this was the burden of the prophet.

CALL TO REPENTANCE

O Israel, return to Jehovah your Elohim; for you have stumbled because of your iniquity. Take with you words and return to Jehovah. Say to him, Remove iniquity altogether; accept that which is good: so will we render the calves of our lips (Hos. 14 : 1, 2).

Hosea's book was not, of course, a continuous narrative, but a collection of the addresses he delivered to his nation, probably compiled by the prophet himself, and there is sometimes quite a hiatus between sections of the book. The last chapter, however, is a logical conclusion to the book.

In his final utterances, he pleaded with Israel to return to Jehovah. The plea was naturally uttered before the Assyrian invasion and prior to the nation being swept into captivity,

165

although the words still have their appeal to the people of Israel today. The words, in fact, form the Haphtarah of Sabbath Shubah, the first sabbath of the Jewish year between Rosh Hashanah and Yom Kippur.

The nation's circumstances and threatened peril should have driven them to repent and to seek Jehovah. His mercy, by implication, was still available to them. They might have to endure chastening for their sins, but ultimate restoration was still possible. It should have been apparent to them that their own guilt was the cause of their stumbling—a term used in respect of a calamity befalling a person. If they realised this, it would be the first step towards reconciliation to God.

A return must be sincere and wholehearted if it was to be effective, and the prophet bade them take with them words, virtually a prayer of confession and of remorse from contrite hearts. Jehovah did not seek offerings or sacrifices but rather the penitential expression of their sorrow at their guilt. Let them, therefore, pray that He might remove iniquity altogether. There could be no approach to God, no communion with Him, while they were still tainted by sin. Only He could cleanse them and free them from their guilt. True repentance implied a definite renunciation of sin and a desire for cleansing.

They should beseech Jehovah to "accept that which is good," said the prophet, that is, the heartfelt repentance and sincerity which He desired to see. Then they would render to Him, not the animal sacrifices they were wont to bring, but the calves of their lips. The Septuagint substitutes "fruit" for "calves" and this is adopted in the A.V. of Heb. 13 : 15. The writer to the Hebrews interpreted the expression as referring to a continual sacrifice of praise to God. It was the rendering of heartfelt worship rather than the sacrifice of animals, and involved an attitude of being which might often have been absent in the presentation of a physical offering.

NO OTHER HELP
Asshur shall not save us. We will not ride upon horses.

Neither will we say any more, Our gods, to the work of our hands. For in thee the fatherless finds mercy (Hos. 14 : 3).

The words which Hosea put into the nation's mouth represented a complete reversal of policy and a renunciation of all other helpers but Jehovah. In their folly the rulers of Israel had intrigued with both Assyria and Egypt, seeking help from first one and then the other. They had relied for security on their negotiations with Assyria and then, in duplicity, turned to Egypt and secured horses and chariots from that country with which to defend themselves (Isa. 31 : 1). Reliance upon Assyria had not helped them and trust in Egypt had brought no guarantee of protection.

They now declared an end to their faithless and reprehensible intrigues. No longer would they trust to Assyria or place any confidence in Egypt. The despicable politics of the court were jettisoned in the realisation of their ineffectiveness.

They had apostasised from Jehovah and served other gods. They had even constructed their own idols and images and acknowledged them as their gods. Never again would they address these idols as their deities: the utter folly of abandoning the true God for objects which they had themselves manufactured was apparent. Henceforth, they had finished with idolatry.

Stripped of the confidence they had had in others, with their human helpers rejected and their machinations now seen as valueless, deprived of the religious support of cult and idols, the nation were as friendless and helpless as penniless orphans. Yet they realised that Jehovah was the God of the fatherless (Psa. 10 : 14) and, in quiet faith, they confessed that in Jehovah the fatherless found mercy.

Unfortunately the confession was never made in Hosea's day, and not until Israel has passed through a still future period of trouble will the acknowledgment of God be wrung from the nation. It is a sad commentary on the intractability of the human heart and its proclivity for rebellion against God.

167

I will heal their backsliding. I will love them freely; for my anger has turned from them (Hos. 14 : 4).

In response to the genuine repentance (presumably still future) of which Hosea spoke, Jehovah responded with alacrity. His people's recalcitrance had demanded His judgment, but immediately there was any sign of contrition, the love of God went out to the penitent heart.

The damage caused to the nation by their backsliding might have seemed irreparable, but Jehovah declared that He would heal their backsliding. He would repair the damage and make whole the wounded body. His love flowed out to them spontaneously and He declared that He would love them freely (literally, as a freewill offering). They had not merited His love but He would bestow it as a free gift.

His anger now had turned from them. The use of terms such as love and anger in relation to God were, of course, pure anthropomorphisms, but they were indicative of the attitude He was prepared to show to His wayward people. When "the time of Jacob's trouble" has ended and Divine mercy has restored the whole of Israel to their own land in a coming day, these words will become true experientially for the nation.

A FLOURISHING TREE

I will be like the dew to Israel. He shall blossom as the lily, and strike his roots like Lebanon. His branches shall spread, and his beauty shall be like the olive tree, and his smell like Lebanon. They shall return and dwell under his shadow. They shall revive like corn and flourish like the vine. Their scent shall be like the wine of Lebanon (Hos. 14 : 5–7).

"The baleful effects of the sirocco," writes Cheyne (*op. cit.,* p. 127), "are often felt in Palestine during the rainless heat of summer, but by the beautiful provision of night mist all hardy forms of vegetable life are preserved." These masses of vapour carried by the westerly winds are the greatest possible boon to the agriculturalist, and Jehovah declared that he would be like the dew, or night mist, to Israel, bringing refreshment in the heat of summer and the necessary moisture for the crops to grow. He would be their sufficiency in every circumstance.

In consequence, Israel would blossom like the lily and strike his roots like Lebanon. The lily multiplies quickly and is the apt symbol of profusion and fruitfulness (cf. Isa. 27 : 6). It has, however, slender roots and quickly withers and dies. But the Divine promise was that Israel should strike roots like Lebanon. The slender roots of the lily would be converted into the strong deep-striking roots of the cedars of Lebanon— or possibly be like the mountain itself. One writer says that "the whole beauty of the promise lies in the paraprosdokian; you expect 'he shall cast forth his roots like an oak or cedar,' but instead of this comes 'like Lebanon', that great Mount Hermon in the Anti-Lebanon which dominates all Hosea's land, the snow-peak which gathers the clouds and devolves the streams, which rests the eyes of weary travellers in the unwholesome plain, and lifts up the hearts of pilgrims to the heavens . . . To be like this deep-rooted, steadfast, far-seen and much loved mountain was better than to be like the fairest of its flowers and the stateliest of its trees (cf. Psa. 92 : 12; Isa. 35 : 2)."

The branches (possibly "the saplings," the same word as in Isa. 53 : 2) would spread, declared the prophet, and the beauty of this incomparable lily would be like that of the olive tree. The olive produces an abundance of silver grey foliage throughout the year (Psa 52 : 8; Jer. 11 : 16) and also a rich crop of fruit, valued as food and also for the oil it produces. Furthermore, the smell would be like Lebanon. The slopes of the pine-clad Lebanon are redolent with the smell of the aromatic myrtles and lavender and the balsamic odour of the cedars (S. Sol. 4 : 11). In a coming day, the beauty and attractiveness of Israel will be fully manifested and the Old Testament predictions will reach their complete fulfilment.

Changing the figure and picturing Jehovah Himself as a great tree, Hosea declared that the people would return and dwell under His shadow. (Some expositors consider the reference is still to Israel and not to Jehovah, but this creates problems in interpretation of the later clauses.) Their trust would consequently find peace, protection and prosperity in Him. There alone can God's people of any day find all their satisfaction and security. Israel would no longer seek security in any other. Jehovah was now their permanent shelter, a condition to be realised fully in the millennial day.

Under His shadow they would revive like sheltered grain. There may also be the implication that, in that safe protection, they would cultivate their grain, free from all disturbance or intervention.

Hosea had previously referred to Israel as a luxuriant vine, bearing wild fruit for herself (Hos. 10 : 1). Now he depicted the nation flourishing like a vine under the shelter of Jehovah. There also their scent would be like the wine of Lebanon. Jewish commentators relate the fragrance to God rather than Israel, but the words seem to apply to the nation itself. Unquestionably everything will be derived from Jehovah, but Israel will produce a scent comparable with the wine of grapes grown on Lebanon.

The whole picture is of a blessed and prosperous nation, enjoying the favour of God, and producing the blossom and fruit, the oil and food which bring pleasure to Him.

IDOLATRY ENDED

Ephraim shall say, What have I to do any more with idols? I respond and look on him. I am like a leafy cypress tree. From me is your fruit found (Hos. 14 : 8).

In the realisation of the wonder of God's grace and all that He had become to His people, Ephraim frankly asked, "What have I to do any more with idols?" Awakening had at last come. The folly of idolatry was now obvious. Only Jehovah was the nation's sufficiency.

At that cry, Jehovah, perceiving that there was now no strange god among His people, answered, "I respond and look on him." There was now nothing to prevent Divine favour being shown to Israel. All barriers to fellowship had gone. By implication, there was a complete surrender to God on the part of the nation and a specific pledge to finish with the old cults and religions. Baalism was at last exposed for its empty unreality. The golden calves appeared as nothing more than inanimate idols. Jehovah was all in all to His people.

Amazingly, Jehovah then declared that He was like a leafy cypress tree, with its perennial greenness. It was one of the most stately trees and its branches swept the ground as though in indication of the grace of God to earth. The earlier imagery had described Ephraim as a tree or plant and it was unusual to find Jehovah depicted in this character. It is, indeed, the only instance in the Old Testament in which Jehovah's relation with Israel was described in this manner (unless poetical passages such as S. Sol. 2 : 3 are interpreted in similar fashion).

In further assurance of His favour, Jehovah declared, "From Me is your fruit found." Some commentators place these words in the mouth of a repentant Israel, declaring that, although the nation had once borne fruit for her own satisfaction, its fruit now was entirely for Jehovah. It is more logical, however, to assume that the words were still those of the Divine Speaker, declaring that all that Israel could desire was discoverable in Him (cf. John 15 : 4, 5).

JEHOVAH'S WAYS

Whoever is wise, let him understand these things: whoever is discerning, let him know them. For the ways of Jehovah are right, and the upright walk in them; but transgressors stumble in them (Hos. 14 : 9).

The prophecy of Hosea not only deals with the ways of Jehovah with Israel, but sets out principles of the Divine dealings with mankind. The prophet, therefore, appropriately

171

called upon the wise to understand the ways of Jehovah as revealed in the book. And he directed the discerning to interpret the Divine principles as a guide for righteous living. As one writer says, "One great mark of 'wisdom' in the Old Testament sense was a rational acquiescence in the equity of the providential government."

The ways of Jehovah become paths to be trodden by the enlightened. They are right or straight paths which lead undeviatingly to the right end. The upright wisely walk in such ways, appreciating that they lead unerringly to the heart of God. To the transgressor, creating his own stumbling blocks by his sin, these ways prove only paths on which he stumbles.

Thus Hosea demands an evaluation of his own book, and the assessment is to be given, not only by a wayward Israel, but by all who read his inspired writings.

BIBLIOGRAPHY

S. L. BROWN: *The Book of Hosea*, 1932.

W. BRUEGGEMANN: *Tradition for Crisis*, John Knox Press, Richmond, 1968.

J. BURROUGHS: *An Exposition of the Prophecy of Hosea.*

T. K. CHEYNE: *Hosea*, Cambridge University Press, Cambridge, 1889.

A. COHN: *The Twelve Prophets*, Soncino Press, London, 1970.

S. L. EDGAR: *The Minor Prophets*, Epworth Press, London, 1962.

H. L. ELLISON: *The Prophets of Israel*, Paternoster Press, Exeter, 1969.

C. L. FEINBERG: *Hosea: God's Love for Israel*, American Board of Missions to the Jews, New York, 1947.

W. R. HARPER: *Critical and Exegetical Commentary on Amos and Hosea*, 1905.

R. L. HONEYCUTT: *Hosea* (Broadman Bible Commentary, Vol. 7), Marshall, Morgan and Scott Ltd., London, 1973.

R. F. HORTON: *The Minor Prophets*, T. C. and E. C. Jack, Edinburgh, 1906.

W. S. HOTTEL: *Hosea—Malachi*, Union Gospel Press, Cleveland.

D. A. HUBBARD: *With Bonds of Love: Lessons from the Book of Hosea*, Wm. B. Eerdmans Publishing Co., Grand Rapids, 1968.

C. F. KEIL: *The Twelve Minor Prophets*, Wm. B. Eerdmans Publishing Co., Grand Rapids, 1961.

W. KELLY: *Lectures Introductory to the Study of the Minor Prophets*, W. H. Broom & Rouse, London, 1897.

G. A. F. KNIGHT: *Hosea*, S.C.M. Press Ltd., London, 1960.

T. LAETSCH:	*The Minor Prophets,* Concordia Publishing Co., St. Louis, 1956.
J. P. LANGE:	*The Minor Prophets,* Zondervan Publishing House, Grand Rapids, n.d.
S. M. LEHRMAN:	*Hosea* (in *The Twelve Prophets,* A Cohn —see above).
H. MCKEATING:	*The Books of Amos, Hosea and Micah,* Cambridge University Press, Cambridge, 1971.
J. MAUCHLINE:	*The Book of Hosea,* 1956.
J. L. MAYS:	*Hosea,* S.C.M. Press Ltd., London, 1969.
G. CAMPBELL MORGAN:	*Hosea: the Heart and Holiness of God,* Marshall, Morgan & Scott Ltd., London, n.d.
J. M. MYERS:	*Hosea-Jonah,* John Knox Press, Richmond, 1960.
A. T. OLMSTEAD:	*History of Assyria,* University of Chicago Press, Chicago, 1924.
E. H. PLUMPTRE:	*Lazarus and other poems.*
E. B. PUSEY:	*The Minor Prophets,* Baker Book House, Grand Rapids, 1970.
G. L. ROBINSON:	*Twelve Minor Prophets,* Baker Book House, Grand Rapids, 1952.
H. W. ROBINSON:	*Two Hebrew Prophets,* Lutterworth Press, London, 1948. *The Cross of Hosea,* 1949.
O. SCHMOLLER:	*Hosea* (in Lange's Commentary—see above).
J. B. SCOTT:	*The Book of Hosea,* Baker Book House, Grand Rapids, 1971.
G. A. SMITH:	*The Book of the Twelve Prophets,* Hodder & Stoughton Ltd., London, 1905.
W. R. SMITH:	*The Prophets of Israel,* A. & C. Black Ltd., London, 1919.
N. H. SNAITH:	*Mercy and Sacrifice: A Study in the Book of Hosea,* Epworth Press, London, 1953.

J. B. TAYLOR: *The Minor Prophets*, Scripture Union, London, 1970.

C. H. WALLER: *Hosea*.

J. M. WARD: *Hosea: A Theological Commentary*, Harper & Row, New York, 1966.

K. O. WHITE: *Studies in Hosea*, Convention Press, Nashville, 1957.

B. E. WOLFE: *Meet Amos and Hosea*, Harper & Sons, New York, 1945.

E. J. YOUNG: *My Servants the Prophets*, Wm. B. Eerdmans Publishing Co., Grand Rapids, 1952.